BRITAIN'S HERITAGE

UNIVERSAL BOOKS LTD

Published 1990 by Universal Books Ltd,
The Grange, Grange Yard, London SE1 3AG
Tel: 01–232 0565
Fax: 01–232 0116

Prepared by Marshall Cavendish Books Ltd,
58 Old Compton Street, London W1V 5PA

ISBN 0 85685 366 6

Printed in Portugal

Introduction

Of the many traces of Britain's rich and varied past to be discovered by the traveller, perhaps the most notable are her castles, cathedrals and gardens. Each has its own attractions, each its own development, but together they catalogue many of the most interesting and fascinating aspects of British history.

Britain's Heritage sets out to explore the outstanding features of each. Starting with castles, it selects over thirty of the most interesting and attractive examples throughout the British Isles, giving the location, the outstanding points of architecture, the splendour of the interiors and the people and events associated with the place. From the tranquility of Dunster to the now ruined Kenilworth with its long and turbulent history; from the sombre walls of the Tower of London to the idyllic beauty of Eilean Donan, a comprehensive text, supported by superb illustrations, gives all the background knowledge necessary to the enjoyment of a visit.

Section two is devoted to cathedrals, and describes their evolution from the original humble religious establishments to the awe-inspiring buildings we know today. From the modernity of Coventry through to Lincoln, perhaps the most exquisite of medieval cathedrals, the superb architecture, the artistry of the workmanship, and the ornate and intricately worked interiors are described in detail alongside splendid illustrations.

The final section deals with perhaps the most renowned aspect of Britain's Heritage, her gardens. Over fifty of the most magnificent and famous of the gardens open to the public are explored, giving special emphasis to unusual or special varieties cultivated, the best time to visit, the background to the design and, in some of the larger gardens, a suggested tour route so that you can make the most of your visit.

As a traveller's handbook or as a reminder of some of the outstanding achievements of Britain's past, *Britain's Heritage* with its wealth of pictures provides a fascinating and concise guide to some of the outstanding landmarks from the past.

Contents

CASTLES:
an introduction

The word *castle* has a definition so broad that it can be used to describe anything from a pre-historic earthwork to a crenellated Victorian mansion. Strictly speaking, however, a castle should fulfil the following requirements: that it is a fortified dwelling, used for defensive and residential purposes.

By the time of the Norman Conquest in 1066 the Anglo-Saxons had been building castles for twenty years. However, these early efforts were soon swamped by the inveterate and almost compulsive castle construction of the Normans.

During the first 50 years of their occupation they constructed more than 100 castles at strategic points up and down the country. Because it was necessary to build quickly these first Norman castles were – for the most part – fairly basic. They were known as *motte and bailey* and consisted of an outer enclosure and an earth mound on which was erected a simple wooden tower surrounded by a palisade. The smallest could be completed within a matter of days while even the largest took only a few weeks.

Yet, even as they built these unsophisticated fortresses, the Normans were acutely aware that they would eventually need something more substantial if they were to keep the Anglo-Saxons in check.

No-one was more conscious of this than William himself. The mighty Tower of London was started within a few months of the Conquest, although he died before seeing it completed, and other great stone castles were constructed around the country during his reign including Colchester, Pevensey and Richmond.

The building of *Motte and Bailey* structures, however, continued well into the twelfth century although they became fewer in proportion to those of stone. In order to build a castle, or to fortify an existing house, it was necessary to be granted a royal *licence to crenellate*. This was not by any means strictly adhered to and when Henry II ascended the throne in 1154 one of his first acts was to destroy large numbers of these so called *adulterines*.

The twelfth century saw the flowering of the keep – massive round or square towers with walls as thick as 20 feet. These either replaced the old wooden towers on the *motte* or were built on new sites. A variation was the shell keep, simply a stone wall thrown around the *motte* to shelter subsidiary buildings. Berkeley, Totnes, Launceston, Cardiff and Usk are all castles which started as shell keeps.

At the same time that keeps were being built, the *bailey* – or outer enclosure – was further protected by stone curtain walls. These usually followed the contours of the land and were lower and not so thick as the walls of the inner area. Eventually, small projecting towers were built along the curtain wall and these, together with a heavily fortified gate house, considerably increased the defensive capabilities of castles of this time.

Towards the end of Henry II's reign the gatehouse was becoming more significant. Designers were realizing that the *outer* defences of a castle should be its strongest point. From 1200 onwards most new castles were provided with hugely strong gatehouses and these, in turn, were often fronted with extra, detached defences known as the *barbican*. The main purpose of the latter was to slow down the enemy's progress by narrowing the approach to the gatehouse.

A typical thirteenth century gatehouse consisted of two round towers, one on each side of the gate itself, which were linked by a chamber, or series of chambers over the gateway arch. Gradually these chambers were used as living quarters, augmenting the somewhat limited accommodation of the keep, and they were by no means spartan.

The next major step forward in castle design and construction began in the last years of the reign of Henry III and reached its ultimate expression through his successor, Edward I. These were the great *concentric* castles, built mainly in North Wales to remind the people of that newly-conquered country that they were now subject to English rule.

Left: The commonest form of Anglo-Norman castle in the eleventh century was the motte and bailey structure. The large mound, or motte, would be surmounted by wooden towers while the bailey, an enclosure on a raised earthen platform, was added to house domestic buildings. The wooden structures were later to be replaced by stone buildings.

Left: The Tower of London combines almost all the styles of castle architecture which have been predominant in Britain throughout the centuries. The innermost building, the Keep, called the White Tower, is Norman and forms the oldest and most important part of the castle, while the remaining defences were built up gradually, the whole being surrounded by a moat.

Caerphilly, completed in the year of Edward's accession, was the first castle of its type to be built in Britain and, covering as it does some 30 acres, is also the largest castle in Wales. Others which followed include Conway, Harlech and Beaumaris, Edward's last Welsh fortress. They all followed the same concentric pattern meaning simply that they consisted of an outer defensive ring of walls, towers and a barbican completely surrounding an inner ring. The gatehouse was built at an angle to the outer barbican, making attack even more difficult.

The end of Edward's reign in 1307 also marked the end of the great castle-building era. The advent of artillery, which could destroy even the most massive fortification, meant there was little point in continuing to build such huge structures. Therefore, throughout the fourteenth, fifteenth and sixteenth centuries the emphasis in castle design tended to concentrate on comfort and amenities rather than thick stone walls.

There was also a realization that sieges were an unsatisfactory and inconclusive

Below: An aerial view of Harlech Castle shows the design of the concentric castle developed in the reign of Henry III but reaching its ultimate expression under Edward I.

way of settling a dispute. Battles tended to take place in the open with armies shifting position rather than remaining in, or around, a static castle.

By the beginning of the sixteenth century many of the old-style castles had been abandoned by their owners. Some attempted to modernize the damp, dark and cramped chambers – occasionally succeeding – but mostly the castles were allowed to decay and crumble.

The new castles built in England were much smaller and designed to accommodate artillery. Henry VIII commissioned many of these new low castles along the south coast ranging from Walmer in Kent to Pendennis in Cornwall.

In Scotland, however, where clan warfare persisted, the chieftains and other landed gentlemen continued to build their castles and towers in the way they had for centuries. These were usually much less sophisticated than their southern counterparts but nonetheless effective: heavy artillery was rarely used north of the border.

However, the Civil Wars of the mid-seventeenth century sounded the death knell for a great many castles. Used either as Royalist or Parliamentarian strongholds, most of them suffered enough during the brief re-emergence of the siege as a method of war and afterwards few escaped Cromwell's vindictive policy of *slighting* – being bombarded or blown up so that never again could they be used as a military garrison.

From this point on, the word castle ceased to have any real meaning. It seemed that every palace, mansion or tower, no matter how luxurious and whether crenellated or not, was called a castle by its proud owner.

But at the same time, particularly during the nineteenth century, serious and laudable efforts were made to restore some of the earlier true castles. There may have been those who wanted to live in a neo-medieval fantasy designed and built for them by a fashionable architect: fortunately for posterity there were – and still are – those who preferred the real thing.

The Civil Wars of the seventeenth century saw the final use of castles in siege warfare and many of them withstood incredible pressure. However, as a result, the Parliamentarians destroyed many to prevent them being used again as a military garrison. Corfe Castle, above, one of the strongest castles to hold out for the King, was nearly totally dismantled as its ruined skeleton today shows.
Above left: Herstmonceux, built in the fifteenth century, was typical of the growing trend away from castles, with all their discomforts, towards the fortified manor house.

Alnwick

Alnwick, the great border stronghold of the Percy family, has been altered, repaired and extended so many times through the centuries that it now presents a bewildering variety of architectural styles.

The first of the major changes was made in 1309 when Henry Percy bought the castle from the Bishop of Durham who held it in trust for the de Vescys, the last of whom was to die at Bannockburn five years later. Between 1309 and 1440 the Percys added seven semi-circular towers, a barbican, two octagonal towers and an impressive gateway, thereby considerably improving upon the basic Norman shell.

Built originally, as were so many of the Northumberland castles and fortresses, to restrain the unruly Scots, Alnwick has had to withstand the effect of siege, the most notable occasion being in 1405 when the castle was taken by Henry IV after the Percys rose up in the rebellion well chronicled by Shakespeare.

However, the Percy fortunes fell into a decline with their adherence to the Lancastrian cause during the Wars of the Roses and their strong Catholic faith during the unrest of the Reformation. In fact, their influence had waned to such an extent that, by 1750, when the estates were inherited by the first Duke of Northumberland, Alnwick was scarcely more than a neglected ruin.

Displaying admirable imagination, the duke sent for the renowned architect, Robert Adam. Adam, undaunted by the complexity of his task, enthusiastically set about the castle's renovation and by 1766, the once decaying pile was transformed into a magnificent ducal residence. Further work was not carried out until the middle of the nineteenth century when the Prudhoe Tower and the chapel were added.

The castle contains an armoury, a museum and a priceless collection of paintings, including examples by Titian, Van Dyck and Canaletto.

Alnwick is situated just off the main A1 road, some 30 miles north of Newcastle-on-Tyne.

Opposite: The Keep and one of the Octagonal Towers constructed during the extensive rebuilding undertaken by the second Lord Percy in the mid-fourteenth century and considered as one of the castle's most impressive features.

Below: Although Alnwick Castle today stands as a magnificent ducal residence, its sturdy outer walls, flanked by sixteen towers, and its strong strategic position act as reminders of the important role it once played as a stronghold in the many border clashes of the fourteenth and fifteenth centuries.

The castle interior at Alnwick forms a fascinating mixture of marvellous design intertwined with reminders of the important role the Percy family have played in British history.
Above: Percy's wallet used to bring news from the Battle of Waterloo.
Right: The splendid interior is a masterpiece of design and includes many famous works of art. The Guard Chamber shown here forms a vestibule to the State rooms of the castle and shows the characteristic octagonal design of many of the ceilings in the castle.

Right: The state coach, built to the order of the third Duke, dates from 1825 and was first used at the coronation of Charles X of France.
Opposite: The exterior of the Keep showing the semi-circular towers and the crouching figures on the battlements thought to have been added in 1765. The cannon in the foreground is one of many on display at Alnwick – some used by the Percy Artillery Volunteers, some captured at the Battle of Vimiero in 1808 and some part of the original armament of the castle.

Arundel

When William the Conqueror created Roger de Montgomery Earl of Shrewsbury, he also made him responsible for maintaining the defences of the Arun valley against sea raiders.

Using the site of an earlier Saxon fortification, Montgomery – anxious to remain in William's favour – built the massively strong castle of Arundel. Fortunately the expected sea attack never occurred and Montgomery enjoyed a peaceful tenure until 1102.

The next occupant, Robert de Belesme, rebelled against Henry I and was able to hold off the monarch's forces for three months. De Belesme had further strengthened the castle by constructing the beginnings of a shell keep. Henry, once he captured the castle, continued the keep while Henry II added the curtain wall and the Bevis Tower.

Arundel then passed into the hands of the Fitzalan family and eventually, in 1580, to the Howards, Dukes of Norfolk. It has remained with the Howards ever since.

The castle suffered considerably in the English Civil War, being pounded by Cromwell's cannon from the roof of the adjoining church of St Nicholas. Roundhead soldiers occupied the castle for five years during which time they caused so much damage that when Charles II handed it back to the Howards, they preferred to live elsewhere.

Desultory repairs were carried out in the early and mid-part of the eighteenth

Left: Arundel, one of the first castles constructed after the Norman Conquest to defend the South Coast, was badly damaged during the Civil Wars. Today only the original shell keep remains.

Below: The interior of the restored Arundel. The castle is now the home of the Dukes of Norfolk, descendents of William de Albini who received Arundel in 1138.

Above: The once heavily fortified gatehouse at Arundel. Constructed by Richard Fitzalan in 1295, the portcullis, drawbridge and the two barbican towers still remain today.

century but it was not until the 1780s that restoration on a major scale began. The tenth Duke spent an incredible £600,000 creating a Gothic fantasy, most of which was dismantled by the fifteenth Duke between 1890 and 1903. He too spent large sums in an attempt to restore Arundel to something approaching its original state.

Arundel is open to the public from April to September on fixed days. Visitors will find the Fitzalan Chapel of particular interest. Built by the fourth earl of Arundel in 1380 it was used as a stable during the Civil War and extensively renovated in 1886.

Balmoral

Balmoral has been a favourite – and private – royal residence since 1852 when Prince Albert, the Prince Consort, bought the estate for £31,500. He demolished a smaller existing mansion and commissioned William Smith, an Aberdeen architect, to build him an imposing new castle in white Crathie granite.

The task took four years and when Smith had finished, Prince Albert and Queen Victoria took possession of a home that the Queen was later to describe as 'this dear Paradise'. The royal couple spent increasing amounts of time in their Deeside haven and when, upon the death of Prince Albert, the Queen went into mourning for virtually the rest of her life, her Balmoral sojourns became so prolonged that the Government of the day expressed grave concern over her continuing absence from London.

The Balmoral estate was once the site of a medieval manor house called Kindrochit, used as a hunting lodge by King Robert II. It then passed through the hands of various owners until in 1845, when the area was first visited by Queen Victoria and Prince Albert, it belonged to Sir Robert Gordon. Three years later, Prince Albert took out a lease on the estate, eventually buying it from the trustees of the Earl of Fife.

Once the original house had been demolished (the site of which is now marked with a stone) the construction of the new castle was started about 100

Below: The royal residence of Balmoral, built by William Smith in the extravagant neo-Gothic manner fashionable during the Victorian era.

Above: The main feature of Balmoral – the 80 feet high square tower topped with a round turret.

yards to the south-east. Prince Albert knew exactly what he wanted: a neo-Gothic extravagance of turrets, towers and castellated battlements. In William Smith he found an architect more than willing to rise to the challenge.

The main feature of Balmoral is an 80 feet high tower, very square, and topped with a round turret and three smaller cone-shaped projections. Inside, the largest room is the ballroom, fully 68 feet long and 25 feet wide. The castle stands in picturesque grounds planted by Prince Albert with rare coniferous and forest trees. Items of interest in the gardens are Queen Mary's sunken garden and Queen Victoria's cottage.

The castle itself is not open to the public but visitors are welcome to the grounds from May to July. Balmoral lies about 35 miles west of Aberdeen in a magnificent setting of forests, mountains and rivers.

Bamburgh

Although the history of Bamburgh Castle dates back as far as the sixth century, nothing now remains from the days when it was the proud seat of the first kings of Northumbria.

The brooding stone pile which stands today on a rocky outcrop dominating the North Sea village of Bamburgh was started in the period following the Norman Conquest; developed during the reign of Henry III; besieged and badly damaged throughout the Wars of the Roses and eventually allowed to fall into decay until the eighteenth century, when it was bought by Lord Crewe, Bishop of Durham.

Some restoration work was carried out but there was still a great deal to be done when the Bishop died, leaving Bamburgh to charity. It then came under the aegis of Dr. John Sharp, Archdeacon of Northumberland.

Dr. Sharp, perhaps best remembered for establishing the village of Bamburgh's first coastguard station, spent much of his own money on the castle. Not only did he restore much of the fabric but he also gave over parts of the castle to practical use, forming a school, a hospital and a library.

In 1838, Bamburgh was the scene of a memorable life-saving drama when the twenty three years old Grace Darling, together with her lighthouse keeper father, rowed out in appalling weather to rescue five people from a wrecked steamboat.

The castle lies about 16 miles north of Alnwick. It contains an impressive armoury and has been used as the setting for many films.

Left: The Keep Hall at Bamburgh. The Keep itself is the least altered part of the castle, its walls varying from nine to twelve feet in thickness and today housing some unusual and fascinating exhibits.

Overleaf: The volcanic outcrop on which Bamburgh Castle stands has long had defensive associations, perhaps dating back to pre-Roman times. The almost impregnable Norman fort, constructed after the Conquest, was subjected to many sieges but it was not until the introduction of artillery that Bamburgh's defences failed and it became the first castle in Britain to succumb to gunfire.

Beaumaris

Beaumaris, silent guardian of the Menai Strait, was the last great castle built in Wales by Edward I. Work started in 1295, employed the combined talents of more than 2,500 men and was supervised – as was usual in this period – by James of St George, Master of the King's Works in Wales.

At this time the threat of rebellion in Wales had receded: Llewelyn, one of the most potent forces, was dead and the latest rising – that of Prince Madoc in 1294 – had been successfully crushed. However, this did not mean that the defences were skimped upon. Far from it. Master James built an immensely strong concentric castle with walls 15 feet thick, surrounded by a moat, and erected two massive gatehouses, one facing the sea, the other the land. This was merely the first stage: twenty years later an outer wall was added. It was not so thick as the inner ring

Left: One of the features of special interest at Beaumaris is the fourteenth century chapel with its lime washed walls and vaulted ceiling.

but had more towers – twelve as opposed to six – as well as two gatehouses, one of which guarded a small dock in the castle's sea-fed moat.

None of these elaborate defences was ever put to the test, although it would have been interesting to see the outcome had they been as, in theory at least, Beaumaris was impregnable. In the unlikely event of the outer wall being breached, the enemy would then have to contend with the much stronger inner wall and the huge gatehouses with their portcullises and double doors.

In 1646, during the Civil War, the castle was a Royalist stronghold. Its defenders were preparing themselves for a long siege when they heard that

Caernarvon had surrendered and that the Parliamentarians had given the Royalists a drubbing nearby. Further resistance seemed hopeless so the commander of the garrison, Lord Bulkeley, surrendered. Fortunately for posterity, Beaumaris was not slighted and is probably the finest example of a concentric castle left standing in Britain. Its fabric is beautifully preserved and is a lasting tribute to Edward I and his Master of Works. A feature of special interest is the small lime-washed chapel with its vaulted ceiling.

The castle is open to the public all the year round and stands on the north side of the little town of Beaumaris.

Below: Beaumaris, the beautiful marsh, is one of the finest examples of a concentric castle in Britain. The almost perfect symmetry could be achieved as, unlike castles of a similar form, the site chosen imposed no restrictions on design.

Berkeley

Berkeley is unique in that it has been inhabited by the same family since it was built – longer than any other castle in Britain – and notorious as the site of Edward II's murder in 1327.

Edward arrived in April of that year and was shut away in a small room, now known as Edward's Cell, in the keep. His gaolers first tried to bring about his death by throwing rotting animal carcasses into an adjoining dungeon, hoping that the King would be asphyxiated by the stench. However, Edward survived this and other deprivations until September when he was murdered in a particularly brutal manner.

Despite this bloody association, Berkeley remains a beautiful, enchanting place. It overlooks, to the west, the Severn vale and is surrounded by terraced gardens, dating from Elizabethan times. Apart from a few additional windows, the castle structure and facade has stood virtually unaltered since the fourteenth century.

From the Thorpe Tower, it is possible to look out over the nearby medieval church, burial place of Edward Jenner, the discoverer of vaccination. The domestic buildings, including the medieval kitchens, are particularly interesting. They are contained within a central courtyard, giving it the appearance of a college quadrangle. The Great Hall, with its open pointed roof and square-topped mullioned windows, is abutted by a fine chapel.

During the Civil War, Berkeley was taken by Cromwell's soldiers after a three day siege. The west wall – as can still be seen – was breached by cannon fire for 35 feet.

Left: In the possession of the same family for over 800 years, Berkeley remains primarily a fortress, being virtually unaltered since the 14th century.

Below: The Inner Courtyard. The distinctive colouring of the castle is the result of a subtle mixture of sandstone and tufa in the walls.

Right: King Edward's Cell where Edward II was imprisoned and eventually murdered. The skull on the table is that of an unidentified young girl, found under the floorboards of the Great State Bedroom during renovation.

Below: The Great Hall displays some of the wealth of tapestries, furniture and paintings to be seen at Berkeley. At the far end is a late sixteenth century screen brought from a Manor House in Monmouthshire during the 1920s. Above, hanging in the Minstrel's Gallery, is a splendid early eighteenth century Gobelin tapestry of the Hunts of Maximillian series. The surrounding pictures are all of various members of the family.

Blair

Blair, with its crow-stepped gable and white-painted towers and turrets, was the last castle in Britain to undergo a siege. This was in 1746 when Lord George Murray, Bonnie Prince Charlie's ablest general, and younger brother of the castle's actual owner – the second Duke of Atholl – tried for seventeen days to capture his family home for the Jacobites.

He failed, as was the whole cause to fail, a few days later in the bloody shambles of Culloden.

The damage caused by this siege and the earlier, but nonetheless lasting depredations of ten years of occupation by Cromwell's troops, prompted the duke to undertake an ambitious re-building programme. He removed the castellations, step-gables and many of the turrets, determined to remodel his home along the lines of a classic Georgian mansion. Sash windows were let into the walls, chimney stacks erected and the oldest part of the castle – Cummings Tower, dating back to 1269 – was lowered.

The duke then turned his attention to the castle interior, creating much of the lavish splendour still standing today. A great staircase was built and the wall lined with family protraits, the most outstanding of which is a full-length painting of the first Marquess of Atholl by Jacob de Witt. The ceiling above the staircase is grandly domed and decorated in stucco.

In 1869, the seventh Duke decided to undo most of his predecessor's work. He wanted Blair to look like a medieval castle again. Accordingly, his architect, David Bryce, master of the revival in the Scottish baronial tradition, rebuilt the

Overleaf: The last castle in Britain to undergo a siege, Blair has suffered considerable damage over the centuries. However, after careful renovation by the seventh Duke, it today stands as a fine example of a Scottish baronial castle.

Below: The Drawing Room at Blair Castle, with its beautifully modelled ceiling and walls hung with crimson damask, is a sample of the magnificent interior. The great wealth of furniture on display in this room includes some fine work by Chippendale.

The Duke of Atholl holds a unique privilege in Britain – the right to retain a private army. Above is a collection of arms and armour assembled over several generations of military campaigns.

turrets and corbels and restored the battlements. Cumming's Tower was put back to its original height and a lofty new entrance hall was installed.

Blair, one of Scotland's largest stately homes, contains a magnificent collection of furniture – including examples by Sheraton and Chippendale – a display of delicate Sèvres porcelain and arms and armour assembled through several generations of military campaigns. Visitors can also see some interesting Jacobite relics, for example Lord George Murray's library.

The castle is finely situated in wooded grounds rising to the commanding rocky heights of Ben-y-Gloe, just off the main road at Blair Atholl, a village on the river Garry. It is still inhabited by the present Duke of Atholl who holds a unique and historically fascinating privilege: the right to retain the only private army left in Britain today – the Atholl Highlanders.

Bodiam

Bodiam, built to act as a deterrent to fourteenth century French raiders, is a fine example of medieval castle building at its best and most imaginative.

Set picturesquely in the middle of a wide, lily-covered moat, Bodiam Castle had lain in ruins from the eighteenth century until it was bought by Lord Curzon in 1917, and lovingly restored to much of its former glory.

Bodiam was built by Sir Edward Dallingrigge and in 1385 he was granted a licence by Richard II to crenellate his mansion, provided that he would then use his fortified home to protect the surrounding countryside. Dallingrigge chose to put a wide interpretation on the conditions of his licence and, instead of crenallating his existing home, began building a castle-proper on a nearby slope.

Mindful of his new responsibilities, Dallingrigge had Bodiam built in such a way that it appeared to be virtually unassailable. The only approach lay across a wooden bridge set at right angles to the main gate. This would leave any attacking force completely exposed on its right flank until reaching an octagonal island in the middle of the moat. From here a drawbridge led to the barbican, or outer defences.

The barbican itself was on an island and if the enemy breached it, they would then have to fight their way across a further two drawbridges and through a succession of portcullises and great doors, before actually reaching the castle itself.

In these circumstances, it is curious to note that on the two occasions when Bodiam was threatened – in 1484 and 1643 – its defenders surrendered with little more than a token resistance.

The main entrance to the castle, with its gatehouse and massive iron-plated oak portcullis, leads directly into the central courtyard, around which the living quarters and other amenities, such as the chapel, are arranged.

The chambers used by the lord and his family were inter-connected. But the quarters allocated to the hired hands had no access to either the family quarters or the gatehouse.

Bodiam is situated about three miles south of Hawkhurst, Kent. It is National Trust property.

Left: Bodiam, built to defend the south coast from French raids at a time when the River Rother was still navigable, lay in ruins after the slighting of Cromwell's men until Lord Curzon, restorer of Tattershall Castle, came to the rescue in 1917.

Overleaf: Bodiam Castle from the south showing the water gate with its machicolated tower.

Braemar

When the second Earl of Mar built Braemar in 1628, he intended it to be used mainly as a hunting lodge. However, with its commanding position high above the River Dee, the castle also presented a warning to the rival Farquharson family that the Mars were well able to defend their territory.

In 1688, when James II fled to France, the then Earl of Mar declared for William of Orange and Braemar was taken over as a garrison for Government troops. But, a year later, giving vent to their long-standing feud, the Farquharsons, Jacobite supporters, attacked Braemar under the command of John Farquharson, a colourful character known as the Black Colonel. The ensuring battle was a rout and the victorious colonel delightedly set fire to the castle.

Braemar languished as a burnt out shell for nearly sixty years. Yet in 1715 it was the scene of a brief flurry of excitement when the sixth Earl of Mar raised the standard on an adjacent mound to launch the first major Jacobite rebellion.

It was not until 1748 that the architect John Adam was commissioned to restore the castle by the Hanoverian Government. By then the castle had actually been taken over by the Farquharsons but they lacked either the funds or the inclination to rebuild this symbol of their old enemy's military might. So the castle was leased to the Government for 99 years at an annual ground rent of £14.

When Adam had finished his task, renovating the interior and adding ramparts, Government troops moved in and stayed there for the remainder of the century. The Farquharsons recovered their property at the expiration of the lease, converted Braemar from a garrison to a family home and took up residence.

The fact that Braemar was always potentially more than a mere hunting lodge can be seen in the massive iron gateway or *yett* and the deep pit-prisons, so characteristic of Scotland's old tower houses. Other points of interest are the star-shaped defensive wall, the barrel-vaulted ceilings, the round central tower and a spiral staircase leading to the principal rooms. The walls of the living quarters still bear the traces of graffiti carved by its soldiers occupants.

The nearby village of Braemar is renowned for the Royal Highland Gathering and in August and September, there is a Son et Lumière at the castle.

Braemar is situated about 40 miles west of Aberdeen.

Below: Braemar Castle, described in 1628 as 'A great body of a house, a jam and a staircase'. Much of Braemar was rebuilt in 1748 by John Adam under the orders of the Hanoverian government.

Right: One of the carved names on a window shutter – a reminder of the time when the castle was occupied by the King's troops.

Right: The entrance to the Laird's Pit, only 12 feet by six, bearing witness to the fact that Braemar was always potentially more than a hunting lodge.

Caerlaverock

Sir Eustace Maxwell must be one of the very few castle owners who made a serious attempt to destroy their own property. In 1312, he was having doubts whether to support the new English king, Edward II, or the forceful Robert the Bruce of Scotland.

When he plumped for the latter, Caerlaverock was immediately besieged by the aggrieved English but managed to withstand the siege. However, in keeping with the Bruce's policy that no building should be left standing that might be of later use to the enemy, he began dismantling his family home.

Fortunately, he did not get very far and thirty-five years later, the damage was repaired by one of his successors. A great deal was added to the castle at this stage: the classic Murdoch's Tower – later the Duke of Albany's prison – the south-east tower and new stretches of curtain wall. In 1355, when held by the English, Caerlaverock fell to Sir Roger Kirkpatrick. He was more successful than the earlier Maxwell, causing so much damage to the castle that it was deserted for the next seventy or eighty years.

Below: The east wing adjoining the gatehouse at Caerlaverock. Although today almost a complete ruin, Caerlaverock once played an important strategic role, guarding one of the most important routes into Scotland.

Opposite: The gatehouse approach to the double drum towers, described as 'the finest example of fifteenth century architecture in Scotland'.

Left: One of the very fine carvings that still decorate Caerlaverock, believed to be a result of the great French influence on the building.

Caerlaverock dates back to 1290 although its origins are fairly obscure. In appearance it resembles one of Edward I's great fortresses and, guarding as it did a Solway Firth landing place, it was certainly as strategically placed. But whoever built it, English or Scots, it was the English who carried out the first of the castle's five sieges: Edward I himself in 1300.

The commanding feature of Caerlaverock is still its mighty gatehouse. This was defended by a 40 feet wide moat and could only be approached over a drawbridge. Elsewhere the castle was surrounded by marshy woodland. The ground floor of the gatehouse was occupied by the guards and the upper storeys contained the main living quarters. These were reached by means of a timber stairway from the inner courtyard.

Various extensions and alterations were made during the fifteenth century but the next major stage in Caerlaverock's development did not occur until 1634 when Robert Maxwell, the first Earl of Nithsdale, built a fine Renaissance style residential block by the east wall. However, he enjoyed his spacious, light rooms for only six years. In 1640 the Covenanters fell on the castle, besieged it for thirteen weeks and then wrecked it so thoroughly that it was never lived in again.

However, the ruins are, in themselves, beautiful and what is left of Nithsdale's interior still bears traces of some fine carvings. Caerlaverock lies seven miles south-east of the county town of Dumfries.

Caernarvon

Since 1301, when Edward I formally presented his son Edward to the people of Wales declaring him their prince, the great castle of Caernarvon has been associated with the title traditionally, but not automatically, bestowed on the eldest sons of British monarchs.

The late Duke of Windsor, then Prince Edward, was invested at Caernarvon in 1911 in a ceremony masterminded by Lloyd George and, fifty eight years later, Prince Charles, the present heir to the throne, was similarly invested.

Caernarvon, a stately ruin, stands on the shores of the Menai Straits, imposing its grandeur on the town from which its name is derived. Work on its construction began in 1283 when Edward I decided the site eminently suitable for another of the castles he was building to impress his authority on the conquered Welsh people. A year later his son was born and, seizing the political expediency of the moment, the king placated the discontented Welsh nobles by presenting the baby as their future monarch, a prince born in Wales and speaking no English.

Work was to continue on the castle for a further 40 years. At first it proceeded at a fine pace, employing the talents of craftsmen and labourers from all over Europe. But, as Edward I's responsibilities elsewhere, particularly Scotland, increased, the flow of funds began to slow down and the work flagged accordingly. When Edward II succeeded to the throne in 1307, Wales seemed peaceful enough; he could see no real need for committing large sums of money to complete his father's fortress. Edward III was similarly disposed and it was not until 1399, in the

Opposite: The towers of Caernarvon are designed so that each one overlooks the adjoining parapet to the next tower. Here, looking across the hollow shell of the castle from the Black Tower to the Chamberlain's Tower, this design is clearly visible.

Below: The irregularly angled walls and the horizontal bands of colour that make Caernarvon distinctive. The shape of the walls was arranged by James of St George, Master of the King's Works, and were thought to be based on the great fortress at Constantinople.

Right: The interior of the Eagle Tower, legendary birthplace of Edward II, the first Prince of Wales.

last year of his reign, that Richard II became the first royal visitor to Caernarvon for 60 years.

By then the castle was no more than a prison for petty offenders. Years of neglect had left their toll: much of the glass, iron and lead had been stolen and all Richard could be offered as a bed was a pile of straw.

In 1403 Caernarvon was attacked by Owain Glendwr. He was repelled by a force of only twenty eight men despite his relentless use of what were then sophisticated siege machines. The castle interior may have been deficient, but the hugely thick exterior walls were impregnable. During the Civil War, Caernarvon was held variously by the Parliamentarians and the Royalists. Charles II's instructions, when he came to the throne, that the castle be destroyed were fortunately not carried out.

In 1908 the Government stepped in and began to restore Caernarvon after centuries of decay. There was little that could be done to improve the ruined interior, but no effort was spared in refurbishing the external fabric. To all outward appearances at least, the castle, with its bands of sandstone and limestone, must now look as it did in the fourteenth century.

One of the most interesting features is the Eagle Tower, popularly supposed to have been the birthplace of the first Prince of Wales, although long disputed in actual fact. It is 124 feet high and houses, in the main room on the ground floor, the laid-up colours of the Royal Welsh Fusiliers. The walls are 18 feet thick at ground level.

The next tower to the south is the Queen's Tower, the Fusiliers regimental museum. From here access is gained to a corridor in the wall which leads, initially, to what was once the great 100 feet long Banqueting Hall. The corridor continues to Chamberlain Tower, which contains the robing room used by the present Prince of Wales during the 1969 investiture, through Black Tower and Cistern Tower to Queen's Gate, the original castle entrance. There are altogether thirteen towers.

The existing entrance is at King's Gate, an elegant loft archway, topped with a seasoned, weather beaten statue of Edward II.

Caernarvon is open to the public all the year round and visitors are allowed to walk along many of the old passages and galleries.

Caerphilly

Caerphilly was the first concentric castle built in Britain and, covering as it does some 30 acres, is also the largest castle in Wales.

Its situation is as awe-inspiring as its proportions. Rising majestically from an island in a vast man-made lake, Caerphilly, even though much of it has crumbled, still seems the apotheosis of a mighty medieval fortress.

The site was chosen by Gilbert de Clare, the Earl of Gloucester, as the perfect position from which to exercise control over the unruly Welsh – in particular Llewelyn, their last great rebel prince. The building began in 1268 but when Llewelyn realized the potential threat of what was obviously going to be a massively strong castle, he attacked the workforce, drove them off and pulled down the rising walls. Nothing daunted, de Clare persisted with his task and the castle was finally completed in 1272.

It was an extraordinary achievement and, with the benefit of hindsight, years ahead of its time. A huge buttressed dam, fully 400 yards long, was built to hold back the waters of the artificial lake thus created. In the centre of the dam is a gatehouse, while at the southern end, a great tower protected the sluices of the Nant-y-Gldyr river which feeds the lake.

Following the island's contours is an outer wall with a gatehouse on the east and west fronts. The inner wall stands 50 feet higher than the outer with four battlemented circular towers at each corner. Its two gatehouses correspond with those on the outside. The main appartments of the castle, including the 70 feet long hall, were contained within the inner ward.

Once Caerphilly was finished, its would-be attackers seemed to accept its apparent impregnability and for many years, few attempts were made to seize it.

Overleaf: Caerphilly Castle, the first concentric castle to be built in Britain and considered almost impregnable. The tower leaning out of the perpendicular was thought to be the result of Cromwell's explosives during the Civil wars.

Below: An aerial view of the castle showing the remarkable engineering feat of the fortified dam, holding the waters of the Nant-y-Gldyr river.

Above: The Keep at Caerphilly. Although allowed to fall into disrepair since the late fifteenth century, much has been done to stop the decay and to preserve the thirteenth century castle.

The first serious assault was made in 1321 when the castle was held by Hugh le Despenser, a favourite of the ill-fated Edward II. Despenser, using his influence with the king, expanded his territory until the patience of his exasperated neighbours ran out and they seized the castle. He was later reinstated by Edward who, five years later, was to seek shelter with Despenser when being pursued by the vengeful Queen Isabella. Her army reached Caerphilly in the winter of 1326, too late to capture Edward who had already fled, but she nevertheless laid siege to the castle. Its defenders refused to surrender until April 1327 when they were finally offered acceptable terms by the frustrated enemy at their gates.

In the fifteenth century, Owain Glyndwr briefly captured and held Caerphilly during the revolt against Henry IV. After that the castle fell into disuse like so many of the other great Welsh castles. By the time of the Civil War it was well on the road to ruin. It suffered the usual ignominious slighting at the end of the fighting and its famous 80 feet high south eastern tower, leaning at least nine feet out of the perpendicular, is believed to be the result of Cromwell's explosives.

In 1949 Caerphilly was taken over by the government as an ancient monument and is now carefully preserved as a building of unique historical importance.

Carisbrooke

One of the most interesting features of Carisbrooke is a well 161 feet deep and the treadwheel used to draw its water. This was once worked by prisoners but their place has now been taken by five donkeys, each of which plods patiently round inside the wheel for two hours a day.

The well is believed to date back to the twelfth century while the wheel itself – designed to reduce the effort involved in hauling the water up from such a depth – did not follow until 1587.

Carisbrooke's most illustrious prisoner was Charles I. He was held here for a year, before being taken back to London at the end of November 1648 to face trial for treason. During his imprisonment, Charles tried to escape twice. The first attempt was a ludicrous failure: he was convinced he could squeeze through the bars of his room, but when he tried he stuck so fast that it was only with the utmost effort that he managed to extricate himself. On his second attempt he was betrayed by a guard whom he had bribed to assist him.

Below: Carisbrooke Castle. The defensive value of the site of Carisbrooke was recognised long before the castle was constructed and today's building still contains traces of the Roman fort built on the same position.

Above: The entrance to the castle through the fourteenth century gatehouse.

Following the sojourn of the Stuart monarch, Carisbrooke became somewhat neglected until Princess Beatrice, Queen Victoria's youngest daughter, succeeded her husband as Governor of the Isle of Wight and made Carisbrooke her home. She lived there for 55 years.

When Princess Beatrice died in 1944, the Governor's Residence was taken over as the Isle of Wight's main museum. It contains various exhibits connected with Charles I.

The castle itself stands on the site of an ancient Roman fort. However, the fort had long since vanished when the land was presented to William FitzOsbern by William the Conqueror. FitzOsbern's son, Roger, was injudicious enough to rebel against the king and, in 1078, was stripped of his possessions, including Carisbrooke.

In 1377 a French invasion force landed on the Isle of Wight but failed to take Carisbrooke. Two centuries later, fearful that Spain would launch an attack, the castle was prepared for war. Luckily the new defences were not needed and instead, the inhabitants were able to watch the pursuit of the Spanish Armada by the English fleet from the castle ramparts.

Shortly afterwards a famous Italian architect and engineer, Federigo Gianibelli, was brought in to strengthen the castle defences even further. His additions included the curtain walls, bastions and bulwarks. Since then, apart from necessary repairs and certain modifications, no further work has been carried out on the castle fabric.

Carisbrooke lies slightly more than a mile south-east of Newport on the Isle of Wight.

Carrickfergus

Carrickfergus remains by far the best-preserved Norman fortress left in Ireland, in spite of having been at the centre of some bloody battles during its long life.

It was built at the end of the twelfth century by John de Courcy, the Earl of Ulster, and became for 300 years the only English garrison north of Dundalk. The castle's construction established the importance of Carrickfergus itself which, until the eighteenth century, was the north's principal town.

In 1210 Carrickfergus was captured by King John and he lived there for a time during his attempt to quell his rebellious knights. Edward Bruce of Scotland attacked the castle in 1315, causing considerable damage and seventy years later the O'Neill of Tyrone tried to burn it down. In 1689 troops loyal to James II tried to hold off the Duke Schomberg but were forced to surrender when he bombarded the castle with heavy artillery.

Carrickfergus was attacked again in 1760, this time by a French naval force. Its defenders fought bravely to their last round of ammunition, then, in sheer desperation, they loaded their muskets with buttons. Finally, when even these were exhausted they resorted to throwing stones. The French commander admired their spirit and treated them with great courtesy when they eventually surrendered. This, incidentally, was the only French victory ever won within the United Kingdom. And it was very short lived. Having provisioned their ships the fleet sailed away to be defeated and captured themselves a little later by a British flotilla.

Carrickfergus was used as a military garrison until as late as 1928 when it became a museum. Most of the items on display are, naturally enough, weapons of war. They include muskets, crossbows and cannon. As well as armour and

Below: Standing on the shores of Belfast Lough, Carrickfergus is probably the best preserved Norman fortress in Ireland, being used as a military garrison as recently as 1928.

Above: Dominating the structure of the castle is the 90 feet high keep supported by walls some nine feet in thickness.

weapons, the museum – situated in the Great Hall – also features exhibits illustrating the history of the Irish cavalry regiments: the Inniskilling Dragoons, the North Irish Horse and the Irish Hussars.

The castle stands on the shore, overlooking the waters of Belfast Lough on three sides and the town on the fourth. There are two half-moon towers on this side with another, between them, over the entrance. The keep itself towers 90 feet, supported by walls nine feet thick. Nearby, in the harbour, a plaque marks the spot where King William of Orange stepped ashore in June 1690, two weeks before the celebrated Battle of the Boyne.

Carrickfergus is open to the public all the year round and is situated about 11 miles along the coast road from Belfast.

Chirk

Chirk was completed in 1310 and has been lived in ever since – although not by the same family. It was built by Roger Mortimer on land received from Edward I as a reward for his help in crushing Llewelyn, rebel Prince of Wales.

Mortimer made himself a massive, square castle with drum towers at its four corners. It seemed more than adequate as a border fortress. Much of this original work still stands today, including two staircases and a particularly large and deep dungeon.

In 1595 Chirk passed into the hands of the Myddleton family and has remained their property since. During the Civil War Sir Thomas Myddleton, a Parliamentarian, saw his castle taken over by the Royalists who retained possession until 1646 when Cromwell ousted them. However, when Myddleton's loyalties switched to Charles I, he found himself as unable to withstand a siege at Chirk as had the previous Royalist forces. He surrendered, fearful that his already much battered castle would be destroyed if he did not.

At the Restoration Myddleton was rewarded for his shifting allegiance when Charles II gave him £30,000. This was used to begin extensive repairs and renovation-work was continued by successive generations of Myddletons.

Chirk is approached through the most exquisite wrought iron gates. These were commissioned in 1718 and completed a few years later by Robert and John Davies, two craftsmen brothers from the nearby village of Bersham. The castle interior contains a long gallery, an old hall, various state rooms, furnishings from the seventeenth to nineteenth centuries and a large number of Stuart portraits, including studies of Charles I and Charles II.

Chirk is open to the public on set days from April to September. It lies four miles south-west of Llangollen.

Left: The exquisite wrought iron gates at the entrance to Chirk Castle. Commissioned in 1718, they were worked by two local craftsmen from the village of Bersham.

Overleaf: The strong rectangular castle of Chirk is set in the heart of a land which, in the turbulent thirteenth and fourteenth centuries, was beset by habitual raiding and skirmishing.

Conway

From the exterior, Conway Castle – like Caernarvon – appears intact. Inside, however, it is a ruin. But the massively thick walls and the eight great drum-towers still stand as firm as when they were first erected towards the end of the thirteenth century.

Conway is approached across the River Conway by one of Thomas Telford's first suspension bridges. Built in 1826, the bridge is now no longer open to vehicular traffic but can be freely used by pedestrians. Its replacement, to the north, was built in 1959. To the south of Telford's bridge is another fine example of nineteenth century engineering: the tubular railway bridge built in 1848 by Robert Stephenson. There are magnificent views of both the castle and the estuary from the suspension bridge.

Conway was one of Edward I's most expensive projects. He wanted the castle

Below: Looking across Telford's suspension bridge, built in 1826, towards the massive exterior of Conway Castle. Designed to overawe the people of Wales, it was constructed at huge expense in the remarkable time of five years.

built quickly and concentrated the efforts of some fifteen hundred labourers and craftsmen to achieve his desire. As a result, Conway was substantially complete within five years but at a cost which even by thirteenth century standards was enormous.

Edward was able to test the strength of his new concentric castle when, in 1294, he was besieged there by Welsh rebels. He had arrived at Conway, ahead of his main force, to personally supervise the quelling of a sudden uprising by Prince Madoc. However, the river was exceptionally full and Madoc – realizing that this would delay the English army – quickly surrounded the castle, hoping to take the king a prisoner. Had the river not subsided within a matter of days, he might have succeeded. Conway was far from properly victualled and the unfortunate English monarch found himself living off bread and water.

In 1399, Richard II was sheltering at Conway, thinking he might be safe there from his cousin, Henry Bolingbroke, Duke of Lancaster. One of his few visitors was Henry Percy, Earl of Northumberland, who persuaded him to leave the castle and promised him safe conduct on the road back to London. Duped by Northumberland's assurances, Richard left the security of the castle and was captured within a few miles. Before the year was out he was dead and Bolingbroke sat on the throne as Henry IV.

Conway then fell into disuse and by 1628 was so dilapidated that Viscount Conway was able to buy it for the trifling sum of £100. During the Civil War John Williams, the Archbishop of York who had been born in the town of Conway, took over the castle and began renovating it at his own expense, intending it as a Royalist garrision. However, in 1646 Conway was captured by the Parliamentarians and Williams's expenditure had been in vain.

At the Restoration in 1660 the castle was handed back to the third Earl of Conway. However, it was in such a bad state that the Earl started its demolition. Luckily he went no further than removing the lead, timber and iron from the interior, leaving the castle shell reasonably intact.

In 1953 Conway became Government property, passing eventually to the Department of the Environment. As such it has been the subject of careful restoration work. One of the most impressive features of the now almost empty interior is a stone arch, one of eight, which once supported the roof of the Great Hall.

Conway is open to the public throughout the year and is situated on the south-east edge of the town.

Right: The interior of Conway is little more than a ruin, although some restoration has taken place. Shown here is the site of the Great Hall with one of the arches, now restored which played an integral part in the design.

Far right: An aerial view of Conway shows the almost triangular plant of the castle, determined by the outcrop on which it stands.

Craigievar

Scotland is a land of beautiful castles but few are as breath-taking as Craigievar, undoubtedly the finest example of Scots baronial architecture still standing.

This remarkable seven-storey castle was completed between 1610 and 1626 by the Bishop of Aberdeen's brother, William Forbes – otherwise known as Willie the Merchant. When he bought the Craigievar estate from the Mortimer family they had started to build the castle, but were forced to abandon the project through lack of funds. Mr Forbes spared no expense in finishing it to his own taste, employing every kind of craftsman in the building of a castle that would outshine all others

They provided him with incomparable plaster moulded ceilings – especially in the Great Hall which also retains its timber screens and a huge fireplace, surmounted by an armorial tablet of the Royal Arms and an inscription which reads: "Doe not vaiken sleiping dogs". A musicians' gallery is situated around the hall. Every room in the castle – including those used by the servants – was built to the highest standards and furnished and decorated in the same way. A particularly fine example is the Queen's Bedroom with its canopied bed and exquisitely moulded ceiling.

From the outside Craigievar has remained unchanged since that day in 1626

Right: Part of the lavish interior at Craigievar. William Forbes spared little expense on the interior of his castle and the best craftsmen were employed to provide him with a castle which would outshine all others.

Opposite: Craigievar Castle, one of the finest examples of Scots baronial architecture still in existence. Not completed until 1626, a period when most castle building in Britain had come to a standstill, Craigievar's seven storey tower house and windows set high above ground level are characteristic of this period.

when Forbes must have stepped back to admire his handiwork. There is only one entrance: a great studded door while, in common with other castles of this type, the first windows are sited high-up to prevent any enemy access through them. The sheer faced walls, in their soft-coloured granite blocks, rise majestically to the roof of cone-shaped turrets and the square central tower with its elegant classical balustrade.

Forbes lived only a year after completing his masterpiece. But he had created a castle which would be admired for centuries to follow. Craigievar remained in the hands of his family – which became, through marriage the Forbes-Sempills – until 1963 when Lord Sempill made it over to the National Trust.

Craigievar is set between the picturesque valleys of the Dee and Don in tree-filled grounds, five miles south of Alford.

Below: One of the most remarkable features of Craigievar is the outstanding plaster moulded ceilings for which the castle is renowned.

Drumlanrig

When the first Duke of Queensberry received the account for his stately new castle on the banks of the River Nith, he was so horrified by the cost that he could not bring himself to spend more than one night there. His successors, however, the Dukes of Buccleuch, had no such qualms and the magnificent pink sandstone building is now happily occupied.

Drumlanrig was constructed between 1679 and 1689 on the site of an older castle. It was popularly supposed to have been designed by Sir William Bruce, the

Above: The ducal coronet surmounting the clock tower.
Left: The North Front and entrance to Drumlanrig Castle. Although in many respects Drumlanrig resembles a stately home more than a castle, it still retains some major castle features including a massive door and a yett at the entrance.

Overleaf: Overlooking the river Nith and set in extensive grounds, Drumlanrig forms one of the first and most important Renaissance buildings in the grand manner of Scottish architecture.

eminent – if somewhat peripatetic – remodeller of Holyrood house in Edinburgh. However, later evidence suggests though while his ideas undoubtedly influenced Drumlanrig's design, the actual architect was James Smith, a young man at the start of a very successful career.

He built the duke a home which, with its sweeping forecourt, wonderfully curved double stone staircase leading up to the broad-terraced entrance, its central clock tower capped with a ducal coronet and its imaginative combination of Renaissance and Castellated styles, looks rather more like a grand country house in England than a baronial hall in Scotland.

The overall effect is one of splendid dignity, especially when glimpsing Drumlanrig and its fifteen lead turrets at the end of the mile-long approach through the rolling hills and wooded slopes, so characteristic of this part of the country.

Inside, the castle is a veritable treasure house of rare and beautiful items collected by generations of the Buccleuch and Queensberry families. There are paintings ranging from gilt-framed miniatures to vast portraits – including studies of King William and Queen Mary on the panelled staircase, which still bear traces of the sword slashes made by bitter Highlanders when they quartered at Drumlanrig on their retreat from Derby during the '45.

The castle, which has accommodated successive members of the Royal Family, also contains a celebrated collection of Louis XIV furniture, silver and various relics of Charles Edward Stuart, the Young Pretender.

Nearby, in the tiny, late seventeenth century parish Church of Durisdeer, there is an elaborate white marble tomb, made by the Flemish sculptor John Van Nost for the second Duke of Queensberry and his Duchess.

Drumlanrig is situated about three miles north of Thornhill, a town long associated with the inhabitants of the castle.

Below: Bonnie Prince Charlie's Room, used by Charles Edward Stuart on his retreat north in December 1745.

Dunluce

Set high on a rocky crag overlooking the sea and reached only by a wooden bridge, Dunluce's picturesque ruins have a mystery and romance all of their own.

The site was once occupied by an ancient Irish fort but the first stones in the existing castle were erected by a Norman, Richard de Burgh, at the end of the thirteenth century. The gatehouse and two round flanking towers are believed to date from around this period while a two-storey Tudor building in the castle centre followed in the late sixteenth century. The money to pay for it came from the proceeds of a Spanish galleon, the Girona, wrecked off the Giant's Causeway in 1588.

In 1639, during a fierce storm, part of the castle collapsed into the sea taking with it a number of servants. By this time Dunluce belonged to the Earls of Antrim and the then Countess refused to live in it any longer. Following the departure of the Antrims, the castle was sadly left to crumble and decay. However, it is still possible to trace the position of most of its halls and chambers.

One of the castle's more interesting features is a sea entrance, a cave down on the shore which connects with the gatehouse. It is thought that the translation of Dunluce – Mermaid's Fort – derives originally from the cave.

A short distance from the castle is another ruin, Dunluce Old Church. In the cemetery surrounding it is buried the crew of the Girona, drowned in the 1588 disaster.

Dunluce is situated midway between Portrush and the Giant's Causeway and enjoys spectacular views along the coast.

Overleaf: The picturesque ruins of Dunluce. Set high on a rocky crag overlooking the sea, the castle became uninhabitable in 1639 when, during a fierce storm, part of the castle collapsed into the sea.

Below: The ruined interior of Dunluce. Once the site of an ancient Irish fort, it was taken over by the Normans during the thirteenth century and later extended by the addition of a two-storey building in the centre during the sixteenth century.

Dunster

Dunster was the last castle in Somerset to hold out for the Royalists during the Civil War. The siege lasted one hundred and sixty days before its defender, Colonel Wyndham, surrendered in April 1646. The usual orders for *slighting* were issued but happily – apart from some minor damage in the lower ward's curtain wall – Dunster escaped relatively unscathed.

Five years later, when Cromwell's soldiers had finished with the castle as a garrison, the owners, the Luttrell family, were allowed to move back, on the payment of a fine for letting the Royalists take over Dunster in the first place. However, it was considered a little enough cost in recovering the home which they and their forebears had lived in since 1376.

Once they were firmly ensconced, the Luttrells devoted themselves to converting Dunster into a comfortable dwelling rather than restoring its former military strength. This work continued throughout the eighteenth and nineteenth centuries culminating, in 1867, with a major re-structuring of the exterior and interior by the eminent Victorian architect, Salvin. This included building a new tower and reconstructing much of the east front in the modern Gothic style.

The beginnings of the castle go back as far as the eleventh century. An entry in the Domesday Book reads: "William of Mohun holds Torre, and there is his castle". Later Mohuns extended and strengthened William's hilltop fortress, although today nothing is left from those early days, except one round tower and a few fragments of wall.

The male Mohun line died out in 1376 and his widow sold Dunster to the Luttrell family, who hold it to this day. One of the first major tasks carried out by the new owners was building – in the early fifteenth century – the imposing gatehouse outside the lower ward. This is three storeys high and features, over its front arch, an intricately carved heraldic panel bearing nine shields.

In 1589 George Luttrell pulled down much of the medieval facade of the

Below: Dunster has enjoyed a period of tranquillity almost unrivalled by any other castle in Britain. The roots of this castle go back as far as the Domesday Book but now little remains of the earlier castle, much having been restructured by the architect Salvin in the nineteenth century.

Above: Set on a hill and surrounded by woodlands, Dunster was one of the last castles in the West Country to hold out against the Parliamentarians during the Civil War.

inner ward residential buildings, replacing them in typically Elizabethan style. His own shield is fixed over the main door which leads into the castle's portrait lined outer and inner halls, the magnificent carved staircase and the banqueting hall decorated with leather hangings.

The next alterations took place in 1765 when the battlements were added to the thirteenth century towers. Dunster was then left in peace until 1867 and the arrival of Mr Salvin.

Dunster stands on a wooded hill, surrounded by well planned gardens and overlooking the village of Dunster which, with its Elizabethan houses and eight-sided Yarn Market, has often been described as the prettiest village in Exmoor.

Eastnor

The most impressive feature about Eastnor is its great hall – a vast room fully 60 feet long, 30 feet wide and 55 feet high. The walls are hung with three-quarter suits of armour, lined with standing suits and decorated with an extraordinary range of weapons, including swords, maces, pistols, daggers and halberds.

The castle itself, although a startling assembly of battlements, towers and ivy-covered stonework, was not built until 1812. It was designed by Sir Robert Smirke, who had already gained a considerable reputation as the architect of Covent Garden, and was later to design the British Museum. The owner, the second Lord Somers, wanted something both extravagant and elaborate: in short, he commissioned Smirke to build him a medieval castle.

Stones were dragged by mules from the Forest of Dean at huge cost; an ornamental lake was scooped out of the ground and cast-iron stanchions were

Below: Eastnor today is as renowned for its beautiful gardens as for the castle itself. The grounds contain many rare plants, trees and shrubs – many of which were planted by the third Lord Somers on his return from foreign travels.

Above: With its many turrets and battlements, Eastnor appears as the epitome of the medieval castle. However, it was not constructed until 1812, in the fashionable neo-medieval style of the nineteenth century.

used for the roof trusses because of the chronic shortage of wood caused through the Napoleonic war effort.

The Somers family went to great lengths to ensure that the interior of Eastnor matched its striking facade. One of the most spectacular achievements is the Gothic drawing room designed by Augustus Pugin, the architect responsible for the interior of the Houses of Parliament. Pugin gave them a room which seems to symbolize some romantic dream: soaring gilded fans, intricate carved capitals, heraldic devices – which adorn every flat surface – and an imposing barrelled ceiling. The whole is illuminated by the light from magnificent brass chandeliers, displaying to full advantage French Gobelin tapestries and an Aubusson carpet.

Another fine room is the Long Library, designed by G. E. Fox in the style of the Italian Renaissance. It is hung with Flemish tapestries while the ceiling is decorated with paintings of the Virtues and Vices. The dining room boasts paintings by Kneller, Lely and Van Dyck.

The gardens and grounds which surround Eastnor are a constant delight. They are stocked with rare plants, trees and shrubs – many of which were planted by the third Lord Somers on his return from travelling abroad in the mid-nineteenth century.

Eastnor, which enjoys breathtaking views of the rolling Malvern Hills, especially the area around the British Camp, an ancient earthwork castle, is open to the public from May to September. Party viewing can be arranged by appointment. It stands two miles to the east of Ledbury.

Edinburgh

Edinburgh Castle, set four-square on a towering volcanic rock, dominates the city, proudly and majestically proclaiming its unassailable position as the premier fortress in the land.

The castle's thousand years of history are as closely interwoven with the pattern of Scotland's progress, as is the Tower of London with England's capital. Believed to be the most popular tourist attraction outside London, Edinburgh Castle has been altered and added to so many times in its long life – particularly during the seventeenth century – that its main features are now historical rather than architectural.

The oldest part of the castle and, in fact, the oldest building in the entire city, is the tiny chapel of St Margaret, dating from the late eleventh century. It commemorates Queen Margaret, the sister of Edgar Atheling, king-elect of England following the death of Harold at the Battle of Hastings. Her chapel was the only part of the castle which Robert the Bruce allowed to remain standing when he captured the fortress from the English in 1313.

Outside the chapel door stands a massive, intimidating cannon known as Mons Meg. When first forged this awesome fifteenth century weapon could hurl a five hundredweight stone ball for more than a mile-and-a-half. Next to the chapel, in the Palace Yard, is the sobering Scottish National War Memorial. It contains the names of 100,000 Scots who perished in the First World War. Opposite is the Great Hall, built by James IV in the sixteenth century, now housing a collection of arms and armour. On the east side of the Yard is the Royal Palace where, in 1566, Mary, Queen of Scots gave birth to James VI who was eventually to succeed Elizabeth I as James I of England.

The Scottish state regalia: crown, sceptre and sword, are kept in the Crown Room, a bomb-proof vault underneath the palace. The crown was last used for

Left: Each autumn, during the Edinburgh Festival, the castle provides a splendid backdrop to the Military Tattoo, held on the castle esplanade.

Opposite: The premier fortress in Scotland, Edinburgh Castle stands on a towering volcanic rock dominating the city.

the coronation of Charles II at Scone in 1651. The sceptre was a gift from Pope Alexander VI while the sword, an ornate Italian piece of craftmanship, was presented to James IV by Pope Julius II in 1507.

Although Edinburgh Castle has never succumbed to actual open assault, over the centuries its stones have received a terrible battering from various 'engines of war'. In 1650 Cromwell's artillery bombarded the castle for three months. The occupants surrendered only after Cromwell threatened to blow up the rock with a mine. Forty years later the castle was besieged for the last time when the Duke of Gordon held it for James II against William of Orange when starvation and disease forced him to capitulate.

In 1745 when the English were in occupation, they chose to surrender immediately rather then attempt to repel Bonnie Prince Charlie's triumphant Highland army.

Since then the castle has been used as a garrison and – during the Napoleonic wars – as a gaol for French prisoners. Examples of their graffiti can still be seen, scratched into the walls of the Casemates, huge vaulted rooms under the Great Hall. No monarch visited Edinburgh again until George IV came north in August 1822 to woo his Scottish subjects.

In 1861 a practice began which continues to this day: the firing of the cannon every weekday on the castle ramparts to mark 1 p.m. This is the Edinburgh citizen's most effective time check.

Each autumn, during the world-famous Edinburgh Festival, the gently-sloping castle esplanade is given over to the military tattoo. This highly popular event attracts visitors – and those taking part – from all over the world.

The view from the castle is unrivalled. The whole of the city is spread out below while, looking north, over the blue waters of the Firth of Forth, it is possible to see the far hills of Fife; from another corner the view takes in the gently rolling Pentland Hills and the route south down towards the Borders.

Edinburgh Castle stands at the top of the city's most historic street, the Royal Mile.

Below: The Honours of Scotland, the Scottish State Regalia. The crown was last used at the coronation of Charles II, as King of Scotland, at Scone in 1651.

Eilean Donan

Eilean Donan, surely the most romantically set castle in Scotland, and certainly the most photographed, stands just offshore on a rocky islet where the sparkling waters of the Lochs Duich, Alsh and Long meet and mingle. The islet is connected to the mainland by a stone-arched causeway but at low tide it is possible to walk across from the shore.

The origins of the castle, now a clan war memorial and museum, go back as far as the Picts, who are believed to have built a vitrified fort on the site. The castle as we know it today was not, however, constructed until 1220 when King Alexander II of Scotland needed a deterrent against the Danish and Norse raiders.

Thereafter it passed into the hands of the MacRaes, the hereditary Constables of the MacKenzies of Kintail, later to become the Earls of Seaforth.

Eilean Donan stood firm and strong for five hundred years until, in 1719, it was pounded to pieces by a British warship. The Jacobites, attempting the second of their three ill-fated rebellions against the Hanoverians, occupied the castle when blown off-course en route from Spain to Inverness. Three hundred Spanish troops and a party of the rebel Highlanders – including the famous Rob Roy MacGregor – garrisoned themselves at Eilean Donan until bombarded into submission by HMS Worcester.

The castle then lay in ruins until 1912 when Colonel John MacRae, a direct descendant of the last Constable, began the restoration that was to take twenty years and cost nearly £25,000. Faithfully following the original design, Colonel MacRae has created a fitting memorial to his clan and ancestors.

Eilean Donan, with its spectacular views of the western approaches to Skye and the Cullins, is situated near the little holiday village of Dornie.

Below: The sad ruins of Eilean Donan Castle, photographed circa 1885. Bombarded into submission in 1719 by an English frigate, it lay almost totally destroyed until its restoration in 1912.

Overleaf: The breathtaking view over Eilean Donan Castle. Set at the meeting point of three sea lochs (Long, Duich and Alsh), the site has long defensive associations, dating back to the Picts.

Left: The faithful restoration has followed the original castle design in detail. The strong entrance and the massive walls were almost impregnable before the use of gunpowder.

Below: The courtyard of the castle. Once having gained entry within the castle walls, any attacker would then have to negotiate the steep staircases, each one guarded by a turret.

Glamis

Glamis is perhaps best known today for its association with the Royal family. The castle was the childhood home of Queen Elizabeth, the Queen Mother and the birthplace – in 1930 – of Princess Margaret, Countess of Snowdon.

The history of Glamis, however, dates back as far as the eleventh century when the site was used as a hunting lodge for the Scottish kings. The first castle was not built until 1372 when King Robert of Scotland granted the lands to Sir Robert Lyon, on the occasion of his marriage to Joanna, the king's daughter. There are still one or two remnants from this period: the Old Kitchen, Duncan's Hall and the Crypt. But Glamis in its present form was not built until the seventeenth century when Patrick Lyon, the Earl of Strathmore, remodelled his family home in the style of a French chateau.

Today it stands, a riot of towers and turrets, set amidst a formalized park of trees, shrubs and broad, sweeping lawns. A feature of the main lawn is a splendidly ornate sundial with carved facets for each month of the year and, altogether, eighty four dials. It was placed there in 1680 and stands a full 21 feet high, supported by rampant lions and twisted pillars.

The castle itself contains innumerable secret passages and there are eerie tales told of the ghosts who wander through the rooms and chambers. A legend has persisted for many years of some hideously deformed creature, apparently born to an earlier Countess of Glamis and locked away for fifty years. The screams of his ghost are still said to be heard ringing through the castle at night.

Many kings and queens have stayed at Glamis. In fact, James V lived there for four years after he had seized Lady Janet Douglas, widow of the Earl of Glamis in 1540, dragged her unceremoniously to Edinburgh, flung her into prison and finally had her burnt at the stake as a witch.

Twenty years later James' daughter, Mary, Queen of Scots stayed at Glamis.

Below: The main entrance to the West Front showing the family crest carved above the doorway.

By then an inquiry had found the charges of witchcraft against the wretched Lady Janet false and the castle was accordingly restored to the Lyon family.

The remodelling began in the early seventeenth century and was to continue for many years. Italian craftsmen executed the magnificent plaster work on the ceiling of the new drawing room on the second floor; a panelled chapel was added, as well as a new west wing and the central tower was raised. Further additions and alterations followed in the nineteenth century, including an extension to the east wing.

Glamis contains various relics: a tartan coat, sword and silver watch belonging to the Old Pretender; a menu written in French for the visit of Mary, Queen of Scots; a fine collection of paintings, furnishings, armour, old documents, jewels and tapestries.

The castle – which Shakespeare linked with Macbeth and the murder of King Malcolm II – is situated five miles west of Forfar.

Above: The Drawing Room at Glamis, designed during the extensive remodelling of the early seventeenth century. The large portrait shows Earl Patrick, the Earl responsible for the rebuilding, with his sons pointing to the castle in the distance.

Overleaf: Glamis today. Although the lands have been in the Lyon family since 1372, the present castle, in the style of a French chateau, was not remodelled until the seventeenth century.

Harlech

Harlech, with its commanding views over the sea on one side and the peaks of Snowdonia on the other, is undoubtedly the most picturesque of the concentric castles built by Edward I to maintain order in his newly conquered principality of North Wales.

It was built towards the end of the thirteenth century by James of St George, the master mason entrusted with the construction of every one of the king's Welsh castles. He employed nearly one thousand men on the project which, when completed, seemed virtually impregnable. The main feature was – and indeed still is – the massive twin-towered gatehouse, the back of which extends some distance into the inner ward, or courtyard.

In 1290, James of St George was appointed Harlech's first Constable. He lived in the gatehouse guarded by a system of portcullises and seven 'murder holes' through which missiles or boiling liquids could be dropped on any would-be attacker. James spent three peaceful years at Harlech, leaving his successor to fend off an assault by the rebel Prince Madoc in 1294.

Madoc found his efforts useless against Harlech's thick walls, moat and precipitous slopes. Its defenders – although only thirty seven strong – were easily able to keep him at bay and, when help arrived by sea from Caernarvon and Conway, Madoc had to admit defeat.

The castle was then used as a prison but, through lack of maintenance, fell into decay. In 1401 it faced its second trial. This time, however, there was no help from the sea and Harlech was surrendered to Owain Glyndwr after a long siege. He then took the castle over as his headquarters and conducted his long rebellion from within its walls. But in 1409, while Glyndwr skulked hopelessly in the hills, the English once more took possession of Harlech.

During the Wars of the Roses the castle was held by Dafydd ap Ieuan, a staunch Lancastrian. He and his men suffered extreme privations – inspiring the marching song *Men of Harlech* – before surrendering to the Earl of Pembroke.

Harlech's last ordeal was during the Civil War when it was held for the Royalists. Even though the castle was, by then, in a sorry state, its defenders were the last to surrender to the Parliamentarians. The usual slighting did not, happily, take place.

In 1914 Harlech was taken over by the Government who embarked on a programme of careful restoration. The interior is now no more than a carefully preserved ruin but the gatehouse still looks as massive as it did in 1290. The outer walls with the Weathercock Tower, Garden Tower, Chapel Tower and Prison Tower at each corner, present an ageless durability very obvious to the visitor who walks along them.

Harlech is open to the public all the year round and lies at the edge of the town of the same name.

Left: The most picturesque of Edward I's Welsh concentric castles, Harlech stands high on a rocky outcrop with commanding views over the sea to one side and the peaks of Snowdonia to the other.

Overleaf: One of the most outstanding features at Harlech is the massive twin-towered gatehouse built with the dual purpose of providing both a defended entrance and quarters for the occupants.

Hever

Hever, once the home of the ill-fated Anne Boleyn, the second wife of Henry VIII and mother to Elizabeth I, was being used as a working farmhouse as late as 1903.

It was then bought by William Warldorf Astor who spent four years and employed the services of two thousand workmen, in restoring the castle to much of its former splendour. He panelled the interior walls, refurbished and redecorated the fine old rooms, and transformed the surrounding gardens from an untidy sprawl into an ordered Italian display of lakes, sculptured fountains, marble statues and exquisite topiary work.

Hever will always be associated with the Bullen family (Boleyn being a more elegant form of the name) whose rapid rise to prominence through a series of marriages reached its height with the marriage of Anne Boleyn to Henry VIII. After Anne's execution, Hever was appropriated by the Crown and, apart from a brief sojourn by Anne of Cleves, was used as a home farm and dairy until bought by W. W. Astor. In May 1983, the house and grounds were purchased by Broadland Properties, owned by the Guthrie family of Yorkshire who continue the tradition begun by the Astors of regarding Hever as a family home.

The thirteenth century castle still retains its moat, crenellated battlements and its imposing south-facing, three-storeyed gatehouse with a square turret set at each corner. On the west side of the castle can be seen some well-preserved chimneys and machicolations – openings in the floor of a projecting parapet through which defenders could shoot or drop missiles vertically on attackers below.

Hever, three miles south-east of Edenbridge, is open to the public from April to October. No admission to the castle is allowed without having first paid for entry to the gardens and grounds.

Overleaf: Hever Castle seen across the moat from the south west. Probably originally designed as a fortified farmhouse, it grew in magnificence with the visits of Henry VIII and the growing fortunes of the Bullen family during the sixteenth century.

Left: The Long Gallery at Hever Castle. During the sixteenth century this would have been used for judicial and social events and the panelling still dates from this time. Today, it houses an exhibition of costumes from the film 'Anne of a Thousand Days'.

The gardens at Hever were transformed during the early part of the twentieth century, much use being made of the water nearby and statuary collected by Mr Astor during his service as American minister in Rome.
Right: The formally planted Rose Garden.

Below: The Piazza overlooking the Great Lake.

Inveraray

Although badly damaged by a recent fire, Inveraray, set on the shores of Loch Fyne, is still one of Scotland's most beautiful castles.

It is the family seat of the Dukes of Argyll and headquarters of the Campbell Clan – still best remembered for their slaughter of forty unsuspecting Macdonalds at Glencoe in the bleak winter of 1692.

The existing castle replaces an earlier fifteenth century building – although some ruins remain nearby – and was started in 1743 when the third Duke commissioned the architects Roger Morris and William Adam to build him a magnificent new home. Unfortunately both Morris and the duke died before their work was completed. The fourth Duke showed no particular inclination to finish the task, and it was left to his successor to employ John Adam and Robert Mylne between 1772 and 1782 in order that Inveraray be properly completed.

It was money well spent. The castle interior, with its ornamented ceilings and magnificently decorated rooms is an extravagance of Gothic splendour. Portraits by Gainsborough, Raeburn, Ramsay and many more, line the walls while elegant pieces of furniture, tapestries, plate and other decoration make a delicate contrast with the displays of armour and weapons.

Among the more interesting items which can be seen at Inveraray is Rob Roy's sporran and dirk handle. The legendary bandit's home lies roughly five miles away, at the Falls of Aray in Glen Shira. A more poignant relic is the cap worn by the eighth Earl and first Marquess of Argyll at his execution in 1661. He had

Overleaf: The blue-grey building of Inveraray is an early example of Gothic revival architecture. Built between 1743 and 1782, today it is the family seat of the Dukes of Argyll and the headquarters of the Clan Campbell.

The tragic fire in November 1975 destroyed much of Inveraray's magnificent interior and today, work is still continuing in an attempt to restore it to its former spendour. Below: The Tapestry Drawing Room before the fire.

Above: In contrast to the stately atmosphere of the rest of the castle, the Armoury Hall contains an amazing collection of various armaments including muskets from the '45 rebellion, broadswords and targes.

supported Cromwell during his suppression of the Highlands and subsequently paid the full penalty when Charles took the throne.

The village of Inveraray itself was destroyed by the Royalist Marquis of Montrose in 1644 but rebuilt by the third Duke when he began his new castle.

The castle is set in attractive, formal gardens and surrounded by some of Scotland's prettiest woodland. A short distance away stands the Aray bridge, an impressive example of John Adam's work. From the bridge – which carries the road between the castle and the shores of Loch Fyne – there are fine views of Inveraray, with its four main towers and multi-windowed facade.

Kenilworth

Kenilworth, once the extravagant home of Queen Elizabeth I's favourite, Robert Dudley, Earl of Leicester, was so severely damaged during the Civil War by Cromwell's vindictive slighting policy, that little now remains except a great empty shell.

A brave attempt was made to repair the castle after the Restoration but the owners were soon forced to admit defeat. Kenilworth was abandoned to crumble still further until 1937 when the then Lord Kenilworth stepped in. Since then it has remained a ruin – albeit an impressive one – but at least its decay has been arrested.

It seems difficult to imagine that in 1575 Kenilworth was the scene of an incredible nineteen day long summer festival, provided by Leicester for the benefit of his illustrious guest, Elizabeth – reputedly costing him £1,000 a day. During his tenure Leicester is said to have spent £100,000 converting the castle from a brooding medieval fortress into a place fit for a Queen.

He replaced many of the narrow Norman windows in the keep with the wider and more fashionable Tudor kind; constructed a new northern gatehouse – known as Leicester's Gatehouse – with four hexagonal corner towers; put up a tall block – Leicester's Buildings – at the south-east corner of the inner ward, containing a number of lavishly decorated rooms, and laid out an extensive pleasure garden, the outlines of which are still faintly visible.

Following Leicester's death in 1588, Kenilworth was inherited by his brother, the Earl of Warwick. He survived Leicester by only a year, however, and his executors later sold the castle to James I for the much under-valued price of £14,000. James handed it to his son, Henry, who used it occasionally as a hunting lodge. Charles I subsequently let it to the Earl of Monmouth but by the start of the Civil War Kenilworth was so neglected that it was already beginning to decay.

Below: Leicester's Buildings, part of the extensive renovation undertaken by the Earl of Leicester for the visit of Elizabeth I in 1575.

Kenilworth was begun in the early years of the twelfth century by Geoffrey de Clinton, Henry I's treasurer. His successors continued the work, erecting the massive Clinton Keep. Henry II decided, towards the end of his reign, that Kenilworth was ideally placed for a Midlands fortress and appropriated it from the Clintons, compensating them with land in Buckinghamshire. Then he, and later King John and Henry III, spent a fortune making Kenilworth one of the strongest castles in the land. Three sides were rendered inacessible by creating a vast artificial lake, the existing defences were considerably extended and five new towers were placed along the outer ward.

In 1266 – just a few years later – Henry was to regret bitterly the effort he had put into strengthening Kenilworth when he found himself on the outside, laying siege to Simon, son of the rebel baron, Simon de Montfort. Even though his father was dead – killed at the Battle of Evesham – Simon held out for eight months. No matter what the king's army used – catapults, hundreds of archers or barges on the lake – it was impossible to take Kenilworth. Eventually Simon surrendered, but only after negotiating a favourable amnesty.

Kenilworth, after one of the greatest sieges in British history, became once more a royal castle. It passed eventually to John of Gaunt, a son of Edward III. He began the work that Leicester was to finish – demilitarizing – and, in doing so, built a great banqueting hall, measuring 90 feet by 45 feet. Unfortunately all that now remains are its roofless but still gracefully decorated walls.

Despite its sorry decline, Kenilworth, lying near the town of the same name, is still a most impressive reminder of medieval castle building skills.

Below: The magnificent porch over the gatehouse at Kenilworth constructed during the rebuilding of the sixteenth century.

Opposite: The ruins of Kenilworth today, severely damaged as a result of Cromwell's policy of slighting after the Civil Wars.

Ludlow

Ludlow, standing high on a hill and dominating the country for miles around, is by far the most important of all the castles built along the border – or Marches –to protect England from the warlike Welsh. Its significance derives partly from its site and – mainly – from the influence of the Mortimer family who took over the castle in the early years of the fourteenth century and held it for five generations.

During the Mortimer's tenure, Edward IV's two sons lived happily at the castle – the north-east tower takes their name – from 1472 until 1483 when they left for their mysterious death in the Tower of London. Seemingly unperturbed by such a sinister association, Henry VII later presented Ludlow to his son Arthur who laid out the terraced walk around the castle for his wife, Catherine of Aragon. The north-west tower, where he died in 1502, commemorates this elder brother of Henry VIII.

The earliest building at Ludlow was carried out by Roger de Lacy towards the end of the eleventh century. He was exiled for rebelling against William Rufus and the castle eventually became Crown property. An early royal tenant was Sir Joyce de Dinian. He greatly extended Ludlow and built one of its most notable features: the round chapel of St Mary Magdalen. The chapel, which was fairly well preserved until the end of the eighteenth century, has a particularly fine entrance and the interior, now open to the sky, once boasted elaborate wood carvings.

The existing gatehouse was built next to the twelfth century keep in 1581 by

Below: Built high on the hill, the massive red sandstone castle of Ludlow dominates the country for miles around.

Sir Henry Sydney, Lord President of the Council of Wales. Sydney was responsible for many extensions and alterations, including the repair and remodelling of the decaying keep intended for use as a prison. When he died he was buried in a magnificent tomb in a church adjacent to the castle.

During the Civil War the Royalist held Ludlow suffered less than many other castles but its defences were dismantled in 1651. The castle was then abandoned to the vandals who stripped all the lead from the roof of the main buildings. By 1811, when it was taken over by the Earl of Powis, Ludlow was just an empty shell.

The most imposing buildings still standing are the Two Princes Tower and Arthur's Tower. Between them is the Great Hall, a magnificent room 60 feet long and 30 feet wide. The adjacent State Apartments contain well decorated, spacious rooms.

Ludlow stands at the edge of the town from which it takes its name.

Above left: Although Ludlow escaped the slighting that destroyed so many other castles during the Civil Wars, its defences were dismantled and the castle left to vandals. By 1811, when taken over by the Earl of Powis, it stood merely as an empty shell.
Top: The view from the castle walls, overlooking the River Teme.
Above: An ivory carving still to be found in the now ruined castle.

Pembroke

Pembroke's great round keep – the finest example of such a structure left in the British Isles – dominates both the castle and the surrounding countryside.

The keep towers 75 feet into the air and is supported by walls which, at the base, are 19 feet thick. It is so massive that it survived Cromwell's slighting during the Civil War, unlike other parts of the castle which now lie in a state of well-preserved ruin.

Apart from the keep, Pembroke's most interesting feature is a vast natural cavern under the north side of the inner ward. The cavern, known as the Wogan, is 70 feet long and 50 feet wide. It was reached originally by a stairway from above, or by water below. It opened out into a creek, large enough for the boats necessary to supply the castle.

Pembroke is built on a steep-sided rock, its outer walls following the contours. There was a castle of sorts on the site towards the end of the eleventh century but the keep itself was not erected until 1200. It was built by the Marshall family, the first Earls of Pembroke and became, with the later additon of a gatehouse, towers and the outer bailey, by far the strongest fortress in South Wales.

In 1457 Henry Richmond who was to become Henry VII, Britain's first Tudor monarch, was born at Pembroke. When at the age of 15 he found himself the main Lancastrian contender for the throne, he was forced to flee to France to escape the Yorkists as they besieged the castle. Fourteen years later, however, he returned and marched with his army to Bosworth where he defeated Richard III, the last Plantagenet king.

Henry's special attachment to Pembroke led to the castle and the town becoming very much associated with royalty especially when Henry conferred the earldom of Pembroke on his son, Henry VIII. But, by the start of the Civil War in 1642, the local residents had become disenchanted with monarchs – Charles I in particular – and Pembroke declared for Cromwell, the only town in Wales to do so. The castle was duly garrisoned by the Mayor, John Poyer, and held out for four years. Then, during the second phase of the Civil War in 1648, Poyer inexplicably switched his allegiance to the Royalists.

Within a short time an army had gathered at Pembroke and the situation became so serious that Cromwell himself travelled to South Wales to conduct the siege. Poyer held the Parliamentarians in check for seven weeks, surrendering only when enemy guns cut off the water supply by smashing the creek entrance to the Wogan cavern.

During the subsequent fighting the Barbican Gate, five towers in the outer ward and the inner curtain were blown up. Of the two towers along the inner curtain, one – the Prison Tower – is still intact while all that remains of the other – the Horse Shoe Tower – are the foundations.

Vandals completed the destruction started by Cromwell and – with the obvious exception of the round keep – Pembroke is now really no more than a vast empty shell.

Nevertheless, as an example of what was once a virtually impregnable medieval fortress, Pembroke is still worth visiting. It is open to the public all the year round and stands on the town's west side.

Right: The once nearly impregnable Pembroke Castle. Built on a steep sided rock, its keep reaches 75 feet into the air and is supported by walls which, at the base measure 19 feet thick, enabling it to withstand the effects of slighting.

Powys

Powys, a stately building in red sandstone, is as famous for its gardens as for its architecture. The gardens, laid out by the incomparable Capability Brown in the eighteenth century, contain a bewildering variety of trees and shrubs. These include a Douglas fir which, at 181 feet, is believed to be the tallest tree in Britain.

The castle itself dates back to the mid-thirteenth century when Gruffydd ap Gwenwynwyn and his son, Owain, extensively remodelled and extended an older stone fortress, given to them by Edward I in return for their support in his wars against the rebel Welsh princes.

Gruffydd died in 1289 at the then considerable age of 74, leaving Owain to continue the work until the end of the century. By then Powys consisted of an outer and inner courtyard, a round tower and a double-towered gatehouse. It was strong and well fortified: standing as close to the border as it did, Powys lived with the constant threat of marauders.

However, apart from a long drawn out dispute over ownership, little of any consequence occurred until 1587 when the castle was sold to Sir Edward Herbert, one of the Earl of Pembroke's sons.

He began a programme of alterations, intending to convert Powys from a fortress to a comfortable home. But his son, created Baron Powys in 1629, reverted it to a military garrison when he stood for the Royalists in the Civil War. In 1644 after suffering considerably, Powys surrendered to the Parliamentarians.

Later, the third Baron Powys – as well as repairing the war damage – carried on with Sir Edward's original work. This included the construction of a magnificent staircase and the state bedroom. He also commissioned William Winde to start building the remarkable garden terraces, to be completed the following century by Capability Brown. Some of these are 200 yards long and drop down in four stages to a lawn. But, before the restoration was complete, Powys – now a Marquis – fled to France.

The castle then passed to the Earl of Rochford, back to the Powys family in 1714 and finally ended up with Henrietta Herbert in 1801. She married Edward,

Right: The stately castle of Powys. Standing on a crag dominating the crossing into Wales over the River Severn, the castle was, by necessity, strong and well-fortified

Far right: The castle grounds are magnificent, arranged in terraces dropping down to the lawn. The view from the loggia, shown here, overlooks the garden across to the Breidden Hills.

Above: The castle forecourt with the beautiful lead figure of 'Fame riding Pegasus' in the centre.

the son of Clive of India and he took the title Earl of Powys a year later.

Towards the end of the nineteenth century much of the interior of Powys was altered and in 1952 it was given to the National Trust. Since then, apart from routine maintenance, the castle has remained the same.

Its main interior features – all strikingly and imaginatively decorated – are the panelled Elizabethan Long Gallery; the Blue Room; State Bedroom; Grand Staircase; Dining Room; Oak Drawing Room and – of course – the splendid gardens with their terraces, lawns, statues and topiary.

Powys is situated on the south side of Welshpool.

Raby

Tradition has it that the magnificent medieval Raby Castle stands on the site once occupied by a mansion belonging to King Canute. If this is true nothing now remains from that period. However, the builders of the present castle – the Nevilles – were descended from a niece of the eleventh century monarch.

The Neville family maintained their moated home for over 300 years before the 'Rising of the North' cost them their royal favour. They had survived the Wars of the Roses: in fact Ralph Neville played a significant part in placing Henry IV on the throne. But in 1569 they overreached themselves when they joined in the rebellion against Elizabeth I aimed at restoring the Roman Catholic faith.

For the next 60 years Raby belonged to the Crown. It was then purchased by Sir Henry Vane during the reign of James I. His son, also called Henry, held the castle for the Parliamentarians during the Civil War; lost it once to Royalist troops and then recovered it with the help of his brother, Sir George Vane. In 1648 the Royalists began a siege but were unable to breach Raby's defences – in particular its great moat. Sir Henry Vane the Elder, however, did not survive the Restoration, Charles II considered him 'too dangerous a man to live' and he suffered execution on Tower Hill.

An attempt was once made to demolish Raby but was halted before any irrevocable damage had been caused. Since then considerable changes have been

Below: The magnificent medieval castle of Raby is, strictly speaking, a fortified home having been granted a license to crenellate in 1378 during the tenure of the powerful Neville family.

Opposite: The Baron's Hall. Although the castle was changed considerably in the eighteenth and nineteenth centuries, much of the original castle remains.

Right: The Kitchens at Raby. The passage around the edge served a dual purpose in that guards could also patrol along it in times of crisis.

made, especially to the interior, but parts of the medieval castle are still visible, most notably the Great Kitchen and the Servants' Hall.

The entrance to the inner court is through a vaulted gateway known as Neville's Tower. To its right stands Joan's Tower. The largest tower – Clifford's – is at the north-west corner of the castle and has walls ten feet thick, liberally broken by arrow slits. Another major point of interest is the kitchen, big even by medieval standards and containing three wide hearths and a gallery running round the walls.

Raby is surrounded by acres of parkland and the castle itself houses a fine collection of English, Dutch and Flemish paintings, period furniture, exquisitely worked tapestries and a collection of carriages.

Raby lies a mile north of Staindrop on the road from Barnard Castle to Bishop Auckland.

St Michael's Mount

It is popularly believed that St Michael's Mount, the home of one of Britain's most spectacularly sited castles, was once part of the legendary ancient kingdom of Lyonesse which supposedly stretched from Land's End to the Scilly Isles.

The earliest known building on the mighty offshore rock began in 1044 when the pious Edward the Confessor founded a Benedictine priory on its peak. Forty years later the priory was duly recorded in the Domesday Book – as was the fact that its occupants paid no tax. Count Robert de Mortain, the first Norman Earl of Cornwall, then annexed the foundation to the abbey of St Michel in Normandy.

In 1194 the rock was put to military use when Henry de Pomeroy fled there after his involvement in the abortive rebellion against Richard I. He held out for a time but eventually surrendered to the Sheriff of Cornwall. Realizing its fortress potential, Richard created the Mount a royal castle and appointed a resident castellan – but not before he had restored the Prior and monks to their home.

The next time the Mount was used militarily was in 1473. The Earl of Oxford maintained it as a last pocket of Lancastrian resistance during the Wars of the Roses and it was six months before starvation forced his capitulation. At the end of the fifteenth century, the impostor Perkin Warbeck seized the Mount and proclaimed himself Richard IV. He left his wife Catherine within its walls while he marched off on his hapless bid for the English throne.

At the Dissolution of the Monasteries, the Mount and its fortified priory passed into the hands of a series of Cornish gentlemen who were made responsible for its military upkeep. They destroyed much of the original fabric in their efforts to strengthen the buildings even further. During the Civil War the Mount stood for the King but surrendered after a short siege.

Below: St Michael's Mount seen at high tide from the mainland.

Right: An aerial view of the castle, first put to military use in 1194.

Above: The Chevy Chase Room in the castle. The frieze around the room, carrying a field sport motif was bought by John St Aubyn in the reign of Charles II and is believed to be Jacobean.

After the Restoration the Mount was sold to Sir John St Aubyn. He, and subsequent generations of his family, made sweeping changes. However, the fourteenth century chapel remained untouched and the monk's old refectory was still used as a dining room. Elsewhere there was a great deal of additional building, particularly in the mid-eighteenth and nineteenth centuries.

St Michael's Mount lies a short distance off Marazion on the Cornish coast and can be reached either by ferry, or – for three or four hours a day – by walking along a narrow causeway. It contains an interesting collection of armour, paintings and furniture as well as preserving its military character with a battery of eighteenth century six pounders outside the main entrance.

The rock and its buildings are administered by the National Trust and are open to the public for three days a week all the year round.

Stokesay

Strictly speaking, Stokesay is not a castle but a fortified manor house. Its defences are minimal and, happily, were never put to the test, despite the fact that it lies in what was once a dangerous Welsh border area.

Overleaf: The tower and part of the hall seen from the court.

The castle entrance is through a picturesque gatehouse framed in timber. This leads into a walled courtyard, once surrounded by a moat 20 feet wide and six feet deep. The gatehouse itself was built in the seventeenth century to replace the original drawbridge house.

In 1291 Laurence de Ludlow, a rich wool merchant, obtained a licence from Edward I to crenellate Stokesay, which had been built by the previous owners, the de Lacys of Ludlow. Ludlow added a strong tower to the south end of the west front and topped the existing north end tower with a new storey. He also demolished the Great Hall and built one of his own, a magnificent room 51 feet long and 31 feet wide. It boasts particularly fine large mullioned windows and, as can still be seen by the smoke-blackened timbers, was warmed by a fire in the centre of the floor.

The last of the Ludlow males died during the reign of Henry VIII; thereafter Stokesay passed through various hands until coming to rest with the Cravens. They, in turn, let it to the Baldwin family who were turned out by the Royalists during the Civil War.

In 1645, however, the Royalists surrendered Stokesay to the Parliamentarians. They had no wish to test the durability of its obviously suspect defences.The Hereford Cavaliers, garrisoned at nearby Ludlow Castle, made a desperate

Below: The romantic Stokesay Castle takes the form of a fortified manor house but, despite standing on a once dangerous border area, its defences were never put to the test.

Above: Stokesay Castle from the east. The gradual rundown of the castle and its use as a granary has not greatly damaged it and today it forms one of the most attractive of Britain's castles.

attempt to recover Stokesay. However, they were headed off by a Parliamentarian force before reaching the castle and suffered a severe defeat. The Royalists lost one hundred men while another three hundred were taken prisoner.

As customary, Parliament declared that Stokesay be slighted, Fortunately, nothing more serious than the removal of the north tower battlements and the blowing down of part of the courtyard occurred. Shortly afterwards the Baldwins moved back and stayed there until the last of them died in 1706.

Stokesay was then taken over by local farmers. The Great Hall was used as a cart shed; its adjacent chambers as granaries while the basement of the north tower became a smithy.

Since the nineteenth century, however, Stokesay has been properly cared for and well deserves its reputation as one of England's more attractive ancient monuments.

It is open to the public all the year, except Tuesdays and is situated on the road from Shrewsbury to Ludlow, three-quarters of a mile south of Craven Arms.

Sudeley

Were it not for the intervention of two enterprising glove makers early in the nineteenth century, Sudeley, once the home of Henry VIII's last wife, Katherine Parr, would probably be no more than a heap of rubble.

Like so many other splendid castles, Sudeley was ignominiously slighted at the end of the Civil War, losing – to start with – the roof of its magnificent banqueting hall. The castle was then left to moulder uninhabited for two hundred years, until being rescued by John and William Dent. Together with the help of Sir Gilbert Scott – restorer of Gothic churches and designer of the Albert Memorial – they then spent a great deal of money and energy in returning Sudeley to something of its former glory.

Below: The Chapel at Sudeley, set behind Queen Katherine's gardens noted for its yew hedges and elegant terraces.

The restoration continued until the mid-1930s, the work of the Dent brothers being taken over by Mrs Emma Dent, daughter of a Cheshire MP called Brocklehurst. Their descendants – the Dent-Brocklehursts – are now the castle's trustees. Mrs Dent devoted her whole life to Sudeley in a worthy attempt to capture its early spirit.

There was originally a manor house on the site, dating back to the days of Ethelred the Unready. But the building which survives today was started by Ralph Boteler at the end of the fourteenth century. Further construction took place in the fifteenth century by the first Baron Sudeley, an Admiral of the Fleet. A staunch Lancastrian during the Wars of the Roses, he lost Sudeley to Richard III. The castle remained Crown property until the newly-ascended Edward VI gave it to his uncle, Sir Thomas Seymour, on the occasion of Seymour's marriage to Katherine Parr, Henry VIII's widow. A letter written by Katherine, accepting Seymour's proposal is one of the fascinating relics now on display at Sudeley. Others include a lock of her hair; a book inscribed by Henry VIII; Elizabeth I's christening robe; Charles I's waistcoat and Queen Marie Antoinette's bed hangings. The castle also contains an impressive collection of paintings: works by Turner, Rubens, Van Dyck and Holbein being among the most eminent.

Sudeley stands in beautiful and carefully nurtured grounds part of which – Queen Katherine's garden – is noted for its double yew hedges and elegant terraces. Katherine's living quarters, built especially for her, have a cloister leading to the chapel where she now lies. Although the castle was restored only comparatively recently there are still traces of the earlier buildings: a north gateway; part of the inner court's west side; and two towers, Garderobe and Portmane all date from the early fifteenth century. Some fine stained glass also survives, although from a later period.

The castle and its grounds are open to the public from March to October. Special features are the exotic waterfowl; a Son et Lumière and the Emma Dent Collection of Victoriana. It is about a mile south east of Winchcombe.

Below: The tomb of Henry VIII's widow, Katherine Parr, which now lies in Sudeley's chapel.

Right: Although Sudeley has recently been much restored, it still contains fascinating traces of the earlier buildings.

Tattershall

In 1911 Tattershall, once one of the finest medieval brick buildings in England, was in a sorry state. Parts of the facade were cracked or crumbling; much of the interior had collapsed and farm animals roamed freely through the ground floor. Four great sculpted fireplaces – masterpieces of design and craftsmanship – had been ripped from their settings and taken to London where they lay, waiting to be shipped across the Atlantic.

When he heard this, Lord Curzon, lately Viceroy of India, was outraged. He determined to save Tattershall for the nation, intending first to restore it at his own expense and then present it to the National Trust.

He set about the task with commendable zeal: he recovered the fireplaces and resited them; re-excavated the inner moat which had been filled in and carefully concentrated on the interior before turning to the external fabric.

Tattershall is one of the few man-made landmarks in the flat featureless acres of the fens. The view from its ramparts is all-embracing. The village of Tattershall huddles below while in the far distance the three towers of Lincoln Cathedral and the unmistakable Boston Stump – St Botolph's Church tower, Boston – break the broad sweep of the sky.

The existing building stands on the site of a thirteenth century moated castle, built in stone by Robert de Tateshalle. In 1433 it came into the possession of Ralph, Lord Cromwell, Henry VI's Lord High Treasurer. He dug a second moat; demolished many of the earlier buildings and reconstructed others. Then he built the great 100 feet high square tower we know today, using the newly fashionable dark red bricks. These were brought from his own kilns and records show that at least one million went into its construction.

The tower has four storeys and forty-eight rooms protected by walls up to 14 feet thick. The windows are ornate and effective - although would have afforded little resistance in any assault. The first floor contains a large hall with another – the Lord's Hall – on the second.

Tattershall is situated about 12 miles north-east of Sleaford, Lincs.

Below: Standing erect out of the flat featureless landscape of the fens, Tattershall Castle is outstanding as one of the few man-made landscapes in this area.

Tower of London

There can be few buildings left standing which are more redolent of the pattern and progress of British history than the Tower of London.

Erected, in the first instance, by William the Conqueror to impress and subjugate the fierce citizens of London, the Tower has impassively witnessed the passage of kings and queens, the bloody deaths of innumerable alleged traitors and now – today – it sits, just as impassive, its sombre walls resounding to the chatter of visitors who have come to see the armouries, the Yeoman Warders – known as Beefeaters – the resident ravens and, above all, the Crown Jewels.

The oldest part of this complex of buildings, which sits brooding by the Thames next to Tower Bridge, is the White Tower. This massive keep, so named because it was painted with whitewash, is the only surviving part of William I's original fortress. An outer wall was added in 1097 to make it even more impregnable. None of this, however, prevented the Tower's first recorded prisoner, Ralph Flambard, Bishop of Durham, making his escape in 1101 after plying the guards with alcohol.

Richard I carried out further extensions but it was not until the reign of Henry III that the Tower was used as a permanent royal residence. Henry built the circle of flanking towers, restored and refurbished the royal apartments and constructed an elephant house for the creature presented to him in 1255 by Prince Louis of France. The elephant, which lived only a short time, was the first of the royal menagerie, later to be housed in the Lion Tower.

The Tower's most famous – or notorious – entrance is Traitor's Gate, leading directly from the river into St Thomas's Tower. It was through this gate that many notables passed after having been tried and found guilty of treason at Westminster. The young Princess Elizabeth entered the Tower through Traitor's Gate but suffered nothing more than brief imprisonment. Anne Boleyn, Catherine Howard and Lady Jane Grey, however, were not so fortunate.

Opposite: The White Tower, the earliest part of the Tower of London and the only surviving part of William the Conqueror's original fortress.

Left: The execution block and axe on display in the White Tower.

Overleaf: The huge complex of buildings that make up the Tower of London, seen alongside Tower Bridge.

Right: The Traitor's Gate, once used as an entrance for prisoners tried at Westminster, among them Sir Thomas More, Anne Boleyn, Catherine Howard and the Princess Elizabeth.

Top: A Yeoman Warder in ceremonial Tudor dress. Above: St Edward's Crown, which dates from the year 1660 and weighs over five pounds.

The list of those who perished in the Tower is endless. The last person to be judicially beheaded there was Lord Lovat, executed in 1747 for his part in the Jacobite rebellion. However, as late as the First World War, eleven spies were shot in the miniature rifle range beside the Martin Tower. The two young princes, Edward V and his brother the Duke of York, are supposed to have been murdered in the Bloody Tower in 1483. No-one knows by whose order, although Shakespeare would have us believe it was Richard III. In 1674 excavations at the foot of a flight of stairs revealed the bones of two boys. Charles II, assuming them to be the remains of the princes, had them reverently removed to Westminster Abbey.

The Tower's last defensive additions – and various other structural alterations – were made by Henry VIII, but were rendered obsolete by the introduction of artillery. Cromwell demolished the royal apartments, ending the Tower's role as a palace, although Charles II perversely spent the night before his coronation within its walls.

In 1875 the Tower was open to the public for the first time. There was much to marvel at – even if it did not include the royal menagerie, transferred to Regent's Park nearly forty years earlier. The same items are on display today: a magnificent collection of arms and armour – including a full-size suit of armour made for an elephant at the Battle of Plassey in India in 1757; the Crown Jewels, housed in a new top-security setting, and for those who enjoy tradition, the daily ceremony of the keys, enacted each night at ten o'clock when the main gates are locked.

The Tower is open all the year round.

Warkworth

Standing as close as it does to the Scots border and being strategically positioned on a spit of land above a river, Warkworth played an important role in defending the North of England during the twelfth, thirteenth and fourteenth centuries.

It was built in the early twelfth century and captured for the first time in 1173 by the Scots king, William the Lion. Later, the owners, the Clavering family, having isolated Warkworth's obvious weaknesses, strengthened it considerably by replacing its original wooden barricades with walls of stone and by building a great gatehouse and two towers: the Carrickfergus on the south and the West Postern.

Their efforts paid off. In 1327 Warkworth was besieged twice – once under the command of the legendary Robert the Bruce – but the defenders were able to hold the enemy back without too much difficulty. The Claverings were not so

Below: Standing high above the river Coquet, Warkworth once played a major role in defending the north of England during the border wars of the middle ages.

Opposite: The Great Gate Tower. Following the Percys' revolt in 1405, the castle was allowed to fall into ruin and as early as 1608 it was being used as a shelter for farm animals.

successful, however, in other areas and in 1332 they lost their castle to the powerful Percy family. Edward III thought it a suitable reward for the Percy's help in repelling the marauding Scots.

Warkworth has remained the property of the Percys – the head of whom was eventually to become the Duke of Northumberland – ever since.

The Percys were delighted with their acquisition and set about fortifying it even further. They replaced the old keep with a massive new one. It was completely square – each side being 65 feet long – and fitted with a portcullis. The first two storeys contained the Great Hall, kitchen and chapel; the third a room in which to relax. One of the keep walls is decorated with a lion rampant, a feature of the Percy coat of arms, and bears the family motto: Esperance – Hope.

In 1405 the Percys rebelled – yet again – against Henry IV but were forced to surrender when he attacked the castle with cannon. By 1608 Warkworth was being used as a shelter for farm animals and most of the castle has continued to crumble slowly ever since.

Some repairs were, however, carried out at the end of the seventeenth century and today a small part of the castle is still actually habitable, although it is not one of the most interesting features of Warkworth: its eight-chambered underground dungeon.

The castle is situated about seven-and-a-half miles south east of Alnwick, the Northumberland's family seat, and is open to the public all the year round.

Below: The castle Keep, constructed by the Percy family and bearing their coat of arms.

Warwick

Perhaps the best remembered of the long list of those who have inhabited Warwick was Richard Neville, otherwise known as the Kingmaker. He enjoyed a unique position of privilege and power for nearly twenty years before meeting his death in 1471 at the Battle of Barnet.

His successor, the Duke of Clarence, took more interest in the castle. He spent seven years there, adding a tower at the northern entrance before he too met a violent end – allegedly drowned in a butt of Malmsey wine at the Tower of London.

The origins of Warwick go back as far as 915, when Alfred the Great's daughter, Ethelfleda, built a wooden fortress on a mound overlooking the river Avon. In 1068 this fortress, together with the growing township of Warwick, was given to Henry de Newburgh, later to become the first Earl of Warwick. He constructed a stone keep, much of which was destroyed by Simon de Montfort's troops during the barons' revolt of 1264.

The little that was left then passed to the Beauchamp family. They – and their successors – were responsible for creating the walls, towers and hall which still stand today.

Possibly the finest of these exterior features is Caesar's Tower, situated at the east end of the long wall. It rises six storeys and is crowned with an unusual double parapet. At the other end of the wall is Guy's Tower, one storey lower

Below: The magnificent white and gold State Dining Room at Warwick Castle, added in 1770. The room is dominated by the Van Dyck portrait of Charles I with his Master of Horse, although it also contains a Rubens.

than its counterpart, but nonetheless impressive. Both towers made a significant addition to Warwick's already elaborate defences.

The interior of the castle dates mainly from the seventeenth century when James I granted it to Sir Fulk Greville, a wealthy member of Parliament. He lavished a fortune on his new home, turning it from a military garrison into a delightful Jacobean residence.

Throughout the eighteenth century Greville's descendants continued the improvements: they travelled widely, acquiring works of art – including paintings by Holbein and Rubens – and established what is still regarded as one of the best and most comprehensive private armoury collections. The castle grounds were laid out by Capability Brown, the acknowledged master of landscape gardening.

Warwick is open from April to October and lies a few miles south of the city of Coventry.

Above: Warwick's main exterior feature is its two towers, Caesar's Tower, rising to six storeys, and one storey lower, Guy's Tower, added by the Beauchamps.

Overleaf: Warwick Castle situated on a mound overlooking the River Avon. The site has long associations with defence, the first castle believed to have been constructed by Ethelfleda, daughter of Alfred the Great.

Windsor

Opposite: The inner gatehouse (called the Norman gatehouse). However, nothing today remains at Windsor from the Norman period, much being restructured by Edward III.

The royal palace of Windsor, one of Queen Elizabeth II's official residences has, in its long, eventful history, seen more of the pageantry of English monarchy than any other place outside London.

Set on a hill overlooking the river Thames, Windsor – the largest castle in England – gives both an impression of powerful, immovable solidity while at the same time purveying a feeling of aesthetic delicacy. It dominates the landscape for miles around, the massive round shell keep reaching high into the sky, well clear of the lower turrets and towers.

Windsor, standing near the site of a Saxon palace used by Edward the Confessor, was built originally by William the Conqueror, the position being chosen for its strategic importance. Nothing now remains from the Norman period and it was not until the reigns of Henry II and Henry III that the castle, as we know it today, began taking shape.

Their successor Edward III left far more visible traces. Born in the castle itself he was largely responsible for transforming it from a military garrison and prison into a royal palace. He instituted tournaments in 1344 and, three years later, founded the Order of the Garter, limiting it then – as it is now – to no more than twenty six knights. A century later the Order claimed what is perhaps Windsor's finest single building, St George's Chapel, as their traditional place of worship.

The chapel – a classic example of perpendicular architecture at its very best – was started by Edward IV in 1477 and completed about fifty years later by Henry

Below: The Queen's Audience Chamber at Windsor Castle. The State Apartments, although not open when the Queen holds court, contain a priceless collection of armour, furniture and works of art.

VII. Henry VIII, the next Tudor innovator, was responsible for the gatehouse at the main entrance to the castle. Its surface still bears traces of the original decorative detail. Henry's daughter, Elizabeth I, constructed the long gallery leading from the royal apartments down towards the park. It now forms part of the Great Library. Below the gallery runs a terrace with a summer house at one end.

During the Civil War, Windsor was used as a Roundhead stronghold and Charles I was held there pending his execution. While leaving the actual fabric of the castle unharmed, Cromwell's men – acting on behalf of Parliament – removed many of its treasures, either having them sold or melted down.

Following the Restoration, Charles II, displaying a fierce passion for modernity, tore down much of the work of his forebears, destroying many fine features in the castle exterior. He left to posterity, however, the famous three-mile long avenue from the Great Park and an abundance of carving by Grinling Gibbons.

Little of any importance was then carried out until 1800, when George III employed the architect, James Wyatt to restore Windsor to something of its medieval splendour. Wyatt, with his love of the Gothic style, threw himself into the task with great enthusiasm but the work ground to a halt when George III suffered a bout of insanity.

Below: The Long Gallery is hung with an amazing collection of pictures, collected by the royal family over the centuries.

Right: An aerial view of Windsor Castle, surrounded by the town on three sides and the immense park on the fourth.

Above: St George's Chapel, the traditional place of worship for the Knights of the Order of the Garter.

The real task of restoring the castle was left until the 1820s when George IV and Wyatt's nephew, Sir Jeffrey Wyatville, began an extensive programme of decoration, alteration and addition. Wyatville completely reorganized the domestic and state apartments and, most noticeably, added some 30 feet to the great Round Tower, finishing off with the flag turret on top.

The castle stands next to the town of Windsor edged with a park of 4,800 acres. The precincts of the castle are open all the year round while the state apartments, with their priceless collections of armour, furniture and various works of art, are open for most of the year – except when the Queen is holding court.

Among the more interesting items on display is a suit of armour made for Henry VIII; a drinking glass used by Elizabeth I and a pair of bellows said to have belonged to Nell Gwynn.

CATHEDRALS:
an introduction

Below: A typical cathedral built and altered over several centuries. Although not based on any particular cathedral, all the features shown might be found together in the same building. The west front and nave are in the Romanesque style, with round arches, massive walls and small windows. This flourished in England in the 11th century, but had been established in Europe for some centuries previously. The transepts, tower and choir are 'Early English', the first English Gothic style, lighter with pointed arches and tall, narrow 'lancet' windows. East of the altar, the building is Perpendicular, a style not found on the Continent, distinguished by its straight lines.

Today Britain's cathedrals are regarded as much as architectural treasure houses as places of worship. Standing as a lasting memorial and tribute to the skills of a bygone age, they have become part of our cultural heritage, something to be nurtured and well cared for. Yet, it was not always so. The eighteenth and nineteenth centuries saw a spate of restoration, an excess of zeal, with not necessarily pleasing results. James Wyatt, the eighteenth century architect, so drastically 'restored' the work of earlier craftsmen that he was considered later to have done more harm than the efforts of Henry VIII's Dissolution and the Puritan vandals combined.

The mid-nineteenth century, however, saw the arrival of Sir George Gilbert Scott, the most renowned architect of his day. He is probably best remembered for designing the Albert Memorial in London's Hyde Park, but his work on nearly half of the country's cathedrals is of far more importance. Scott gave them a new lease of life. True, there was the occasional stylistic lapse but on the whole he not only managed to undo as much as he could of Wyatt's folly, but also ensured that his own restoration was a genuine attempt to give the cathedral back its former glory.

Most people equate cathedrals with size; they think of York's massiveness or Salisbury's soaring spire, but sheer bulk has nothing to do with it. Quite simply, a cathedral is no more than a church which contains the throne of a bishop. The word itself is derived from the Greek *cathedra*, meaning chair. The cathedral became the centre of the diocese, or area over which its bishop had religious jurisdiction.

Until 1535 all the cathedrals, as well as monasteries and churches, were Roman

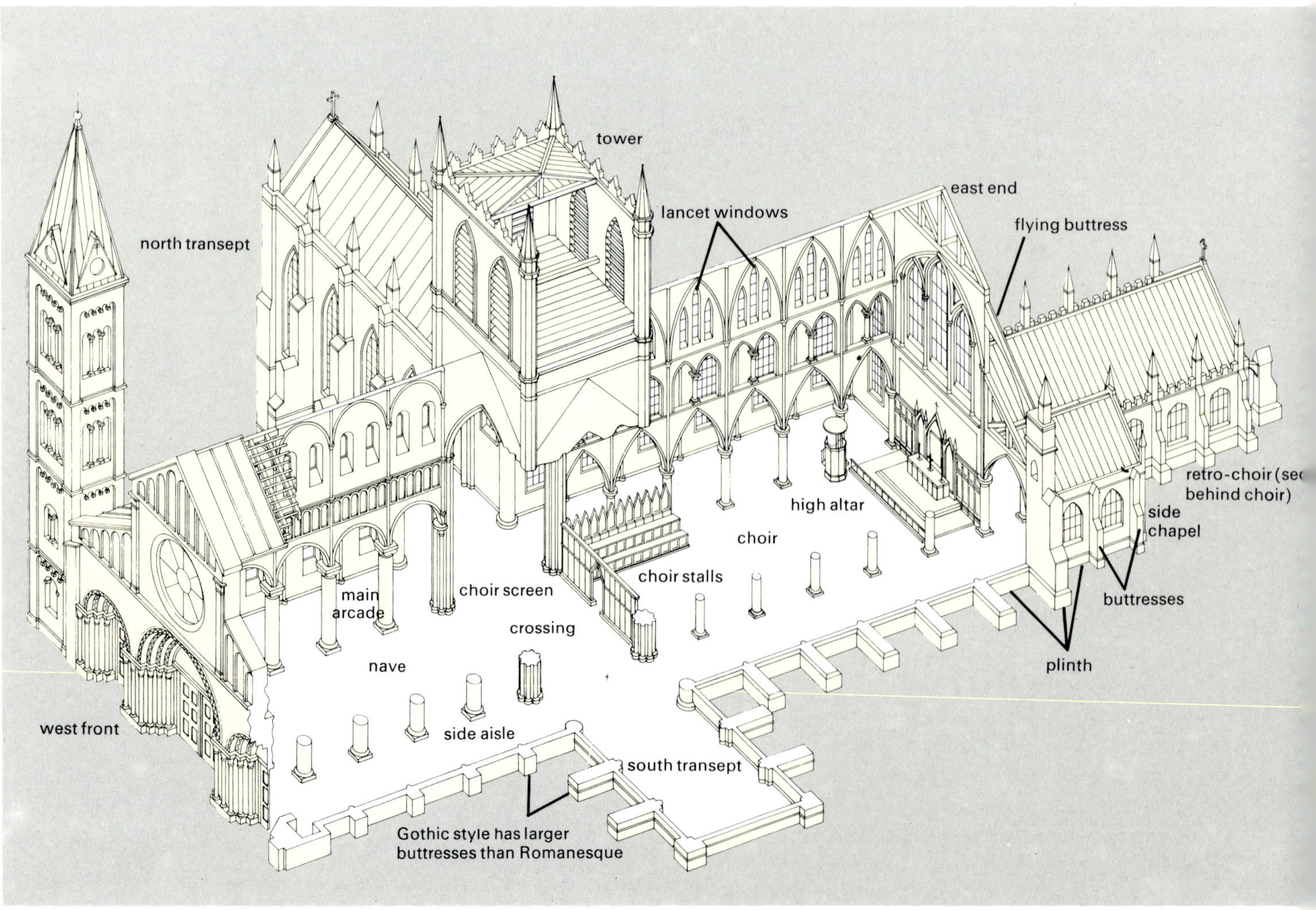

Left: Two outstanding examples of Norman architecture in England. The nave at Ely Cathedral, far left, shows the typical Norman wall-passage above the ground-storey arcade. In this case the roof of the nave is made of wood which is decorated with 19th century paintings. At Durham, left, the masons experimented with rib-vaulting in the nave and choir. The zig-zag carving on the columns was a popular Norman decoration.

Catholic, ruled by the Pope in Rome. The early sixteenth century, however, saw a swelling discontent with the way the church conducted its affairs, seemingly increasing its wealth at the expense of the populace and at the same time blithely disregarding their welfare, spiritual or temporal.

It was in Germany that Martin Luther spearheaded the break with Rome and the impetus soon spread throughout Europe. In England in particular, there was a growth in the new Protestant religion especially among the young intelligentsia. These included men like Tyndale and Coverdale, who translated the Bible into English, Latimer and Cranmer, later to become Henry VIII's Archbishop of Canterbury.

It was against this setting that the English Reformation took place. In order to marry Anne Boleyn Henry VIII demanded that Pope Clement VII should annul his marriage to Catherine of Aragon stating that as Catherine had previously been married to his late brother, Arthur, the marriage was invalid. The Pope refused. As a virtual prisoner of Charles V, the powerful Holy Roman Emperor and Catherine's nephew, he had no choice.

This apparent Papal obduracy gave Henry the excuse he needed. He was well aware of the influences at work in Rome and bitterly resented being subject to the whims of foreign potentates. Over the next five years he gradually cut England off from the Catholic Church in Rome. He declared himself, through Parliament, Supreme Head of the Church of England, stripped the clergy of its power and privilege and dissolved the monasteries.

The Religious Reformation marked the end of one era for the church and the start of another. Henry seized abbey lands and sold them; church interiors were wrecked and most of the precious items removed to the royal coffers. Many of the buildings were destroyed, either merely for the sake of destruction or to provide stone for some secular purpose: Oxford Cathedral is a case in point; it was partially demolished by Cardinal Wolsey so that he could build what was later to become Christ Church College.

Once it was recognized that the Church was now truly subservient to the State, no more building of any importance occurred until St Paul's in the late seventeenth century. There was a flurry of activity in the eighteenth and nine-

Below: Two forms of vault found in cathedrals. The first, a groined vault, a development of the simple Romanesque barrel vault. The second, the fan vault, characteristic of the English Perpendicular style.

Right: The beauty of medieval stained glass windows is a major feature in many cathedrals throughout Europe. The 15th century rose window at St Chapelle is a late form with a 'flamboyant' style of stone tracery.

teenth centuries but this was as much a restoration of the old as it was the creation of anything new.

The mid-seventeenth century witnessed England's Civil War and yet another setback to the great cathedrals and churches. Cromwell's soldiers stabled their horses in the naves, smashed irreplaceable medieval stained glass, tore down statues, wrecked fine old carving and generally caused as much wanton destruction as they could. The cathedral exteriors were, for the most part, spared the indignity of cannon bombardment but, nevertheless, it took the majority of them almost two centuries to recover.

This was as long as some of them had taken to build. The earliest cathedrals, dating from the Anglo-Saxon period, were usually built of timber or in very basic stone. Very few traces of these survive most having been burnt down, devastated by raids or demolished by the Normans.

The Normans were the first to build cathedrals in the grand manner. William the Conqueror replaced virtually all the Anglo-Saxon bishops and appointed his own from Normandy. Each one wanted his own distinctive cathedral, something that would preserve its builder's name for posterity.

Norman architecture, also known as *Romanesque* because of its tendency to follow the Roman pattern, lasted until around 1150. It is characterized by bulk: heavy pillars, thick walls and sturdy semi-circular arches. The design is that of a Latin cross formed by a nave and transepts. There is usually a low, square central tower or twin towers at the west end. Stone vaulting would be used only over fairly narrow stretches and decoration tended to be fanciful and bold.

By the mid-twelfth century *Romanesque* architecture was giving way to *Early English Gothic*. Arches became pointed and pillars tall and slender with stone vaults covering wider sections of the roof. It was all a great improvement on the solidity of the Normans but still lacked overall finesse which followed in the next important development, *Decorated Gothic*. It was an architectural flowering, growing stronger from 1250 to 1350. Design became much more elaborate; parapets and pinnacles appeared, doorways were less recessed, windows were enlarged and given tracery of geometric precision, the nave was usually widened and, above all, the cathedral was filled with exquisite carving.

This was followed by the more straightforward *Perpendicular Gothic*. This developed in the mid-fourteenth century and lasted until about 1540. The Black Death of 1348 had wiped out almost half the population, including the craftsmen engaged in cathedral building and decoration. As a result cathedrals became lighter places. The walls were not so thick, columns were slender, windows were larger, and the emphasis was placed on light, space and a new refined delicacy.

Henry VIII and Cromwell effectively dampened any architectural enthusiasm during the sixteenth and seventeenth centuries and it was 1675 before the foundation stone of St Paul's, England's only cathedral built during this period, was laid. Sir Christopher Wren's masterpiece is built in the *Renaissance* style, the first and last major cathedral of its kind in Britain.

The return to Gothic architecture of the eighteenth and nineteenth centuries both in new building and the restoration of the old has been surpassed by the twentieth century cathedrals. They have no form dictated by time: they can be as traditional as the great Anglican cathedral in Liverpool or as adventurous as Coventry.

Below left: An illustration from a 15th century French bible showing Solomon watching the building of the Temple. It is, in fact, a building of the period, and the picture shows contemporary workers scribing a stone before cutting it to shape, carrying roofing materials up a ladder, hammering roofing lead into place and, in the background, mixing mortar with a wooden shovel.

Below: York Minster was built without proper foundations, being simply supported on thousands of wooden piles driven into the soil. When these started to give way, the only solution was to replace them with modern concrete, but the task was complicated by having to work entirely from underneath to avoid disturbing the fabric.

Armagh
St Patrick's Church of Ireland Cathedral

Armagh is the ecclesiastical capital of Ireland, being the seat of both the Archbishop of the Church of Ireland and that of the Roman Catholic church. Each faith has its own cathedral, each confusingly called St Patrick's.

The history of St Patrick's Church of Ireland Cathedral dates back to the fifth century when it was founded by the saint himself. By the ninth century the building was known locally as 'the great stone church'. However in 1268 the incumbent Primate began an extensive remodelling which eventually absorbed all traces of the earlier work except the arches of the crypt. The existing transepts date from this period. In the mid-fourteenth century St Patrick's was extended further, serving 200 years later as a fortress during an uprising against Elizabeth I. Consequently the cathedral was badly damaged and left a ruin until 1613 when another restoration was started.

St Patrick's is fairly small, just 182 feet long, and is unusual in that the nave and

Below: The original church of St Patrick, founded in the fifth century, has long since disappeared. However, his name has been preserved and the cathedral which occupies the same site today stands as a pleasing tribute to his memory.

Left: The north aisle contains some fine pieces of statuary including the recumbent figure of Dean Drelincourt by Michael Rysbrack, the Flemish sculptor.

choir do not align. This is believed to symbolize the attitude of Christ's head on the cross.

The cathedral houses some fine statues including, in the nave, an eighteenth-century study of Sir Thomas Molyneux by the noted sculptor, Louis Roubillac. There is also a remarkable recumbent effigy of the Dean Drelincourt, sculptured by the Flemish Michael Rysbrack. The moulding on the great west door incorporates an intriguing collection of pagan carvings while high up on the cathedral's exterior walls there is a splendid assortment of medieval carvings.

The Chapter House contains several mysterious stone statues, one of which is thought to be Queen Macha, while the library houses a selection of rare books and manuscripts. The most interesting of these was written in Italian by a fourteenth-century monk, Brother Stephanus, who claimed that is was dictated to him in colloquial Italian by St Catherine of Sienna when he was in a trance. There is also a copy of Gulliver's Travels with corrections by Swift.

Bristol

Bristol is unique in that it is the only English example of what the Germans define as a hall church, that is a church in which the nave, choir and aisles are the same height.

It was founded as an Augustinian monastery in 1140 and consecrated in 1165. Parts of the original building still survive, most notably the Chapter House. Approached through a delightfully dignified Romanesque vestibule this is generally regarded as one of the finest Norman rooms in the country with its remarkable zigzag moulding and interwoven arches lending a special quality.

Another of Bristol's unique features is the fact that it possesses two Lady Chapels. The first of these, the Elder Lady Chapel, was built in 1215 and is situated off the choir's north aisle. It contains a great deal of rich carving on the capitals of the pillars and between the shoulders of the arches. The craftsmen who executed the exquisite detail were on secondment from the great West Country cathedral at Wells.

The Eastern Lady Chapel, conventionally sited beyond the High Altar, followed in the early fourteenth century at the same time as the choir. It too is finely decorated and boasts the first lierne vault in England. The medieval colours of the reredos behind the altar have been carefully restored and it seems to glow with light and warmth. Lining the walls are the tombs of various abbots including that of Abbot Newbury (1428–1473), whose tomb rests in an ornate stellate recess, and the rather bizarre sixteenth-century cadaver tomb of Bristol's first bishop, Paul Bush.

The choir shares the same magnificent lierne vault as the Eastern Lady Chapel and has the tallest arches in England. The aisles feature probably the most splendid stellate recesses in the country as well as an intriguing vault crossed with stone bridges, each bearing three carved heads. Just off the south choir aisle is the sacristy with its elegant roof and the early fourteenth century Berkeley Chapel. This contains the unusual tomb chest of Thomas, Lord Berkeley and his wife. Hanging from the ceiling is a delicately worked medieval candelabrum. It was made in 1460 and is the oldest of its kind in any English church.

Right: This exquisite candelabrum was made in 1460 and is believed to be the oldest of its kind in any English church. It depicts St George slaying the dragon and is surmounted by a figure of the Madonna and Child.

Opposite: Bristol Cathedral's 19th-century west front with its twin towers. One of them contains a peal of bells rescued from Temple Church, Bristol when it was destroyed by bombs in 1940.

Overleaf: The High Altar backed by the intricately carved reredos.

Canterbury

Canterbury, mother church of the Anglican faith and scene of the martyrdom of Thomas Becket, is one of Britain's best known and most visited cathedrals.

Its first stones were laid in 597 when Augustine arrived from Rome with a party of monks to baptize King Ethelbert of Kent. Augustine's cathedral – a simple oblong building with an apse at each end and north and south towers – survived until 1067 when it was gutted by fire.

Undaunted, the first Norman archbishop, Lanfranc, lately Abbot of Caen, began the task of rebuilding. Within a surprisingly short time – seven years – Canterbury once more had a cathedral. It had a central tower, a nave, transepts and twin towers with pinnacles of gold, But in 1174, four years after Canterbury's most famous incumbent, Thomas Becket had been struck down following an injudicious remark by Henry II, windblown sparks and ashes caught between the lead roof and the joists: the lead melted and the building went up in great gusts of flame. Only the nave survived.

Rebuilding took ten years. It was started by a Frenchman, William of Sens, and completed by an English master-mason after William was crippled by a fall. Their most important commission was re-siting the shrine of the now canonized Thomas Becket. This was done by first restoring and then extending the eastern choir. In 1200, amidst a great deal of pomp and ceremony, the saint's remains were

Below: The cathedral from the south east. The porch forms the main entrance for daily use.

Above: The cloister at Canterbury, a fine example of perpendicular lierne vaulting with heraldic bosses commemorating donors to the cathedral's reconstruction.
Right: The exterior of Canterbury Cathedral presents a wide variety of styles which perhaps have little unity but each with its own inherent beauty.
Far right: Canterbury's stained glass is among some of the most remarkable in the world. This thirteenth century window portrays the parable of the rich man.

VLITIVS M VRICIVS

brought up from the crypt and placed in their new resting place – Trinity Chapel – where they were later joined by the magnificent tombs of the Black Prince and Henry IV.

Becket's sumptuous jewel encrusted shrine was to prove one of the cathedral's greatest attractions for the next 350 years as pilgrims poured in from all over the world. But in 1538 Henry VIII declared the saint a rebel and a traitor: his shrine was desecrated and its treasure appropriated for the royal coffers.

Towards the end of the fourteenth century the Norman nave had deteriorated to such an extent that it was pulled down and rebuilt in the early Perpendicular style. It is set at a slight angle to the choir. The great central bell with its exquisite fan vaulted lantern is one of the finest examples of its kind. It is known as Bell Harry – and was built at the end of the fifteenth century in place of the original

Below: Looking east along the splendidly proportioned and graceful nave. Completed in 1410 under the direction of Henry Yevele, Henry IV's master mason, it replaced the earlier and much deteriorated Norman nave.

Above: The choir at Canterbury. Much of the original was destroyed following a fire in 1174 and was restored to its present glory twenty five years later.

Left: One of the Cathedral's most famous monuments, the tomb of Edward of Woodstock, Prince of Wales (1330–76), better known as the Black Prince. The railings enclose a fine effigy of a 14th-century knight, although it is believed not to be the Prince himself.

Angel Steeple. Bell Harry, so named because it once housed a single bell called Harry, has been described as 'the queenliest tower in Christendom'.

Apart from the splendour of the architecture, the tombs, chapels, cloisters and painted panels, Canterbury's most impressive feature is its twelfth and thirteenth century stained glass, undoubtedly the loveliest in Britain. Other outstanding features include the early fifteenth century carved stone pulpitum which separates the choir from the nave; the ancient marble throne of the archbishops, believed to date from 1210; the tomb of Henry Chichele, archbishop from 1414 to 1443 – depicting him both in his splendid vestments and as a wasted naked corpse – and, of course, the Martyrdom where Thomas Becket fell under the swords of Henry II's avenging knights.

Chester

A tenth century Anglo-Saxon church, built to house the relics of St Werburgh, the abbess daughter of a Mercian king, once stood on the site of Chester Cathedral. This gave way to a Norman Benedictine Abbey which was itself rebuilt between the thirteenth and sixteenth centuries.

The first building to be completed was the Lady Chapel. Much of it was restored by Sir Gilbert Scott in the nineteenth century while some of the fittings are even later. At the back stands the sadly mutilated shrine of St Werburgh. It dates from about 1310 and until 1876 it formed part of the Bishop's Throne in the choir.

After the Lady Chapel came the choir. It was built by Richard of Chester, one of Edward I's military engineers in Wales, and contains probably Chester's finest feature, the exquisitely carved stalls. The misericords, small carvings under ledges on which to lean during services, are particularly notable and surpass those in most British cathedrals. The gates to the north and south aisles of the choir are made of sixteenth century Spanish wrought-iron. However, the screen which separates the choir from the nave is a Victorian replacement of one from the Middle Ages.

The nave itself was completed in the sixteenth century and is a mixture of

Left: Standing on the site of an ancient Saxon church, the much restored Chester Cathedral retains its dignity.

Below: The 14th century choir stalls feature some of the finest carved medieval misericords in Britain.

Above: The richly carved and decorated 14th century choir stalls are separated from the nave by a 19th century screen.

Decorated and late-Perpendicular styles. At the west end of the south aisle, in an unfinished Norman tower, is the nineteenth century baptistry. The font, also of the same period, is Venetian. On the other side of the nave, in the base of the unfinished south tower, is the seventeenth century consistory court. The court, with its oak table and screens, was presided over by the Chancellor of the diocese and was used for trying ecclesiastical offences. It is the only example of such a court left anywhere in the country.

Much of Chester was restored in the nineteenth century – not always harmoniously – but the monks' domestic buildings remain almost as they were in the Middle Ages. These are the best preserved monastic buildings in Britain and give a very good idea of what life was like. They are grouped around the cloister on the north side of the cathedral and include the splendid thirteenth century monks' dining hall or refectory. At one end is the stone dais used by the abbot and important visitors.

The oldest surviving part of Chester is a sturdy eleventh century arch and arcade in the north transept, leading from a chapel into the sacristy. Another interesting feature is the thirteenth century chapter house in the Early English style. Its entrance vestibule is particularly charming.

Chichester

The tapering graceful spire of Chichester Cathedral stands as a landmark for miles around. It soars 277 feet into the sky, dominating the west Sussex countryside and the picturesque city below.

Chichester was built towards the end of the eleventh century on the site of an older collegiate church. In 1114 a fire devastated much of the work but builders repaired the damage and by 1184 the cathedral was virtually finished. Three years later another fire broke out, severely damaging the eastern end. Again it was repaired but this time a stone vault was added and extensive alterations were made to the retrochoir. The two bays behind the high altar were completely remodelled in the Transitional style – the period between Norman and Gothic. The result, an impressive combination of Norman severity and Gothic charm, is one of Chichester's outstanding features.

The retrochoir used to contain the shrine of St Richard, canonized in 1262 and thereafter the focus of pilgrims' devotions for 300 years until Henry VIII ordered its destruction.

The addition of chapels to either side of the nave in the thirteenth century made Chichester – with its corresponding double aisles – the third widest cathedral in England. The upper stage of the central tower with its plate-tracery windows also belongs to this period. The spire, rising from the central tower,

Below: The Arundel Tomb, bearing the effigies of Richard Fitzalan, the Earl of Arundel, who died in 1376, and his countess. The tomb stands in the north aisle of the nave. The Earl's feet rest on a lion; his lady's on a dog.

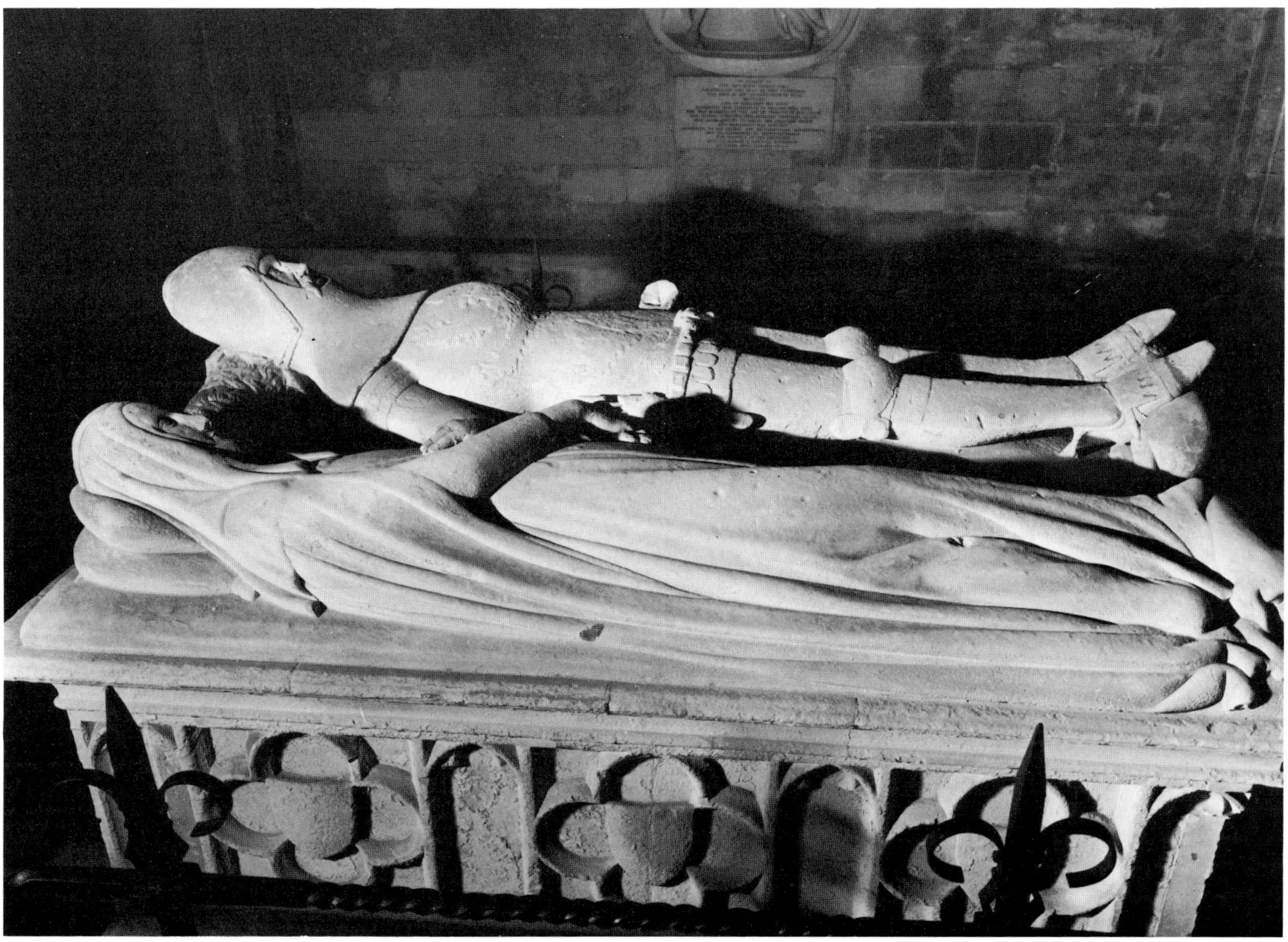

Opposite: Chichester Cathedral from the north-east. The unique free-standing 15th century bell tower stands to the right.

was rebuilt by the eminent Victorian architect, Sir Gilbert Scott, after it collapsed in 1861 following a severe storm. The beginning of the twentieth century saw the rebuilding of the north-west tower which had crumbled and fallen as long ago as 1635.

A unique feature of Chichester is its fifteenth century free-standing bell tower. It contains a ring of eight bells: two from the sixteenth century, three from the seventeenth and three from the early eighteenth.

The cathedral's most precious possession is a pair of twelfth century stone carvings. Originally coloured, these carvings depicting Christ at the raising of Lazarus and at the gates of Bethany, are situated on the right of the south choir aisle. They were placed there in 1829 after having been found behind the choir stalls, and are probably the finest examples of medieval carving in Britain.

One of Chichester's most interesting features is a John Piper tapestry hung behind the altar from a sixteenth century screen. The tapestry, divided into seven strips, symbolizes the Trinity and was installed in 1966 after being woven in France. Another fine piece of modern art is the Graham Sutherland painting of Mary Magdalen and the risen Christ. It hangs in the Mary Magdalen Chapel where it blends well with the altar rails, candlesticks and book-rest cast in aluminium by Geoffrey Clarke.

Among the many tombs and plaques is a marble memorial to the noted eighteenth century Chichester poet, William Collins, and the fourteenth century Arundel tomb which bears effigies of Richard Fitzalan, Earl of Arundel and his countess.

Right: Some of the finest examples of medieval stone carving to be found in Britain are in Chichester Cathedral. This 12th century stone carving of Christ at the raising of Lazarus is one of two carvings in the south choir aisle.

Coventry

Coventry Cathedral is one of the twentieth century's most imaginative, significant and moving buildings. Its combination of a fourteenth century shell and a dramatic new main structure ensure for this – and future – generations its deserved place as a classic architectural concept.

The old cathedral was destroyed by fire one terrible November night in 1940 when the city of Coventry was laid waste by enemy high explosive and incendiary bombs. All that remained after the holocaust were the blackened outer walls and – as if by a miracle – the magnificent 295 feet high tower and spire.

Within sixteen years Elizabeth II laid the foundation stone of Sir Basil Spence's new cathedral – he won the commission in an open competition – and on May 25th 1962 the building was consecrated. It had cost £1,350,000 and during the eight years it took to build there was not a single industrial dispute among its 500 workers.

The cathedral is now almost as well known for the astounding works of art it contains as it is for its design. Undoubtedly the most striking of these is Graham Sutherland's great tapestry *Christ in Glory* set above and behind the High Altar. The tapestry, the gift of an anonymous Coventry citizen, is the largest in the world, 75 feet by 34 feet, and dominates the entire cathedral.

Another immense feature is the curved Baptistry Window. Designed by John Piper and made by Patrick Reyntiens, its multi-coloured glass and patterned mullions represent an abstract ideal of the light of the Holy Spirit. At the foot of this mighty window, which extends from floor to ceiling, is the font. This is a

Right: This unique Cross, made of silver gilt, rests on the hammered concrete High Altar. Behind it is the incomparable Christ in Glory tapestry by Graham Sutherland.

Opposite: The incredible curved Baptistry Window is yet another of Coventry Cathedral's unique features. At its base is the font, a huge, mis-shapen hunk of sandstone.
Overleaf: A dramatic illustration of the combination of old and new; the burnt-out, 14th century shell wedded to the 20th century creation of Sir Basil Spence.

Right: Sir Jacob Epstein's forceful and effective bronze sculpture of St Michael gaining victory over the Devil. It overlooks the main entrance to the cathedral.

rough, mis-shapen sandstone boulder hewn from the Barakat Valley near Bethlehem.

Opposite, on the other side of the nave, is the circular Chapel of Unity. Designed in the form of a crusader's tent, the chapel has long slender stained glass windows and a beautiful mosaic marble floor.

The main entrance to the cathedral – which is built south to north unlike older ones which run west to east – is through the great canopied porch linking the old and new buildings. It is approached from the east up the broad sweep of St Michael's Steps, overlooked by Sir Jacob Epstein's incomparable bronze sculpture of St Michael subduing the Devil.

From the porch the ruins are reached by the Queen's Steps. The sanctuary contains Coventry's most poignant relic: two charred roof beams tied together in the shape of a cross with the words 'Father Forgive' carved into the stones behind. At the foot of the cross is another. It is made from two of the fourteenth century hand forged nails which literally rained from the roof as the old cathedral perished.

Durham

Despite the fact that Durham was largely built in the remarkably short time of forty years it is deservedly regarded as Britain's finest Norman cathedral.

Impressively situated on a rocky hill high above a loop in the River Wear, Durham stands on a site once occupied by a tenth century church built to house the shrine of Cuthbert, the shepherd boy who became a saint.

In 1093 Bishop William tore down the Anglo-Saxon edifice and laid the foundations of the new cathedral. He died three years later leaving his successor, Bishop Flambard, to continue the work. By this time the choir was finished, the stone vaulting in the aisles being the oldest of its kind in Europe. When Flambard died in 1128 no bishop was appointed to take his place for five years. So, during the interim period, the monks themselves took over. By 1133 they had finished

Below: The cathedral cloisters. These were heavily restored in 1827, losing much of their original charm.

the nave, the aisles and the stone vaulting, this last being one of Durham's most outstanding features.

The nave is richly decorated, the great pillars incised with deep channels in a most unusual way. A short distance inside the nave a black marble slab marks the spot beyond which women were once forbidden. St Cuthbert it seemed disliked women and none were allowed to approach his shrine.

Durham owes its development to the veneration accorded to St Cuthbert. At one time his shrine was reputed to be the most magnificent in Christendom, heaped with jewels, silver and gold. All this, however, disappeared in 1540 when the cathedral surrendered to the crown. What remains lies behind the High Altar, a plain stone slab marking the saint's burial place. His coffin was opened several times down through the centuries and each time it was reported that the body lay uncorrupted.

St Cuthbert is also commemorated in a magnificent twelfth century painting hanging in the Galilee Chapel, where it looks down on the sixteenth century tomb of the Venerable Bede – monk, historian and scholar – who died at Jarrow in 735. The chapel was built in the twelfth century and altered in the fifteenth when its graceful marble shafts were joined by those of stone.

The whole of Durham's interior is lavishly decorated although the screen behind the High Altar – presented by John, Lord Neville in 1380 – has now lost the 107 statues it once contained. The choir stalls are three centuries younger and ornately carved.

The Bishop's Throne, reputedly the highest in any cathedral, surmounts the extravagant tomb erected by its occupant, Bishop Hatfield. He presided at Durham from 1318 to 1333.

On the north-west door is an interesting reminder of medieval days: a sanctuary knocker. Criminals clutching at it could claim sanctuary – and immunity for their offence – for up to 37 days.

Opposite and overleaf: 'half church of God, half castle 'gainst the Scot' – Sir Walter Scott's apt description of Durham Cathedral.
Below: The sanctuary knocker. Any criminal reaching it was given immunity for 37 days.

Above: Part of the priceless Anglo-Saxon stole found in the coffin of St Cuthbert, the north country's most renowned saint.
Left: This reclining figure marks one of Durham's many tombs. The adjacent pillars bear indentations peculiar to the cathedral.

Edinburgh
St Giles' Cathedral

St Giles, the High Kirk of Edinburgh, Scotland's capital city, has a history stretching back more than 1000 years. However, it has been greatly altered and restored down through the centuries, not always happily.

If some of its original overall splendour has been lost, St Giles still retains an impressive interior, its celebrated square central tower with the miniature steeple supported by flying buttresses and – above all – an abiding sense of history.

There was a small church here in the ninth century. When the Normans arrived they built their own church which in turn was destroyed in 1385 when Richard II led a raiding party into Scotland. All that was left were the four immense central pillars.

Two years later the rebuilding started and continued until the latter years of

Left: A floodlit view of St Giles's Crown Steeple supported by its flying buttresses.

Opposite: The Thistle Chapel. Built to serve the Knights of the Thistle, Scotland's oldest order of chivalry, it surprisingly dates from only 1911.

the fifteenth century. In 1454 the kirk was presented with a precious relic, the arm bone of St Giles, a French holy man. However, in 1557, following the Reformation, an ornate gilded statue of St Giles was tossed into the waters of the Nor' Loch below the castle. In 1559 the formidable John Knox became minister of St Giles and within a short time all the old Roman Catholic altars and 'graven images' had been swept away. The walls were whitewashed and the kirk subsequently divided into three separate churches. It remained partitioned until 1872. Knox died in 1572 and is buried in a simple grave at the back of St Giles.

A restoration was carried out between 1829 and 1833 but it did more harm than good. Many of the ancient side chapels and a large part of the west section suffered irreparable damage at the hands of the well-meaning but misguided 'restorers'. It was only the later intervention of William Chambers, publisher and Lord Provost of Edinburgh, that saved St Giles from total desolation. His own work was completed in 1883.

St Giles contains innumerable memorials to famous Scots. They include the

Below: St Giles from the west front. It opens directly onto Edinburgh's High Street, better known as the Royal Mile.

Right: The Marquis of Montrose's monument. It was erected in 1888 to commemorate the Captain-General of Charles I's forces in Scotland. He was executed in 1650 after having been found guilty of treason.

Marquis of Montrose's monument in the Chapman Aisle and an elaborate tomb erected for the first Marquis of Argyll, the covenanter who was executed in 1661 a few years after he himself had been largely responsible for the death of Montrose. The Robert Louis Stevenson memorial in the Moray Aisle Chapel commemorates the great writer.

One of the kirk's most interesting features is the Thistle Chapel, built as recently as 1911 and famous as the most ornate building in Scotland since the Middle Ages. It was designed by Sir Robert Lorrimer for the Knights of the Thistle, Scotland's oldest and grandest order of chivalry, and contains some impressive heraldic glass, wood carving and a particularly elaborate ceiling.

There is also a colourful stained glass window near the Albany Aisle. It was made by the pre-Raphaelite William Morris from a design by Burne-Jones.

Ely

When the central tower of Ely Cathedral collapsed in 1322 after standing for more than 200 years it was replaced with a structure that is unique in European cathedral architecture: a great stone octagon topped with a wooden lantern rising from its centre.

Its creator was a man of vision, imagination and engineering ability far ahead of his time. Faced with the gaping hole, Alan of Walsingham, the sacrist, decided against restoring the original tower, opting instead for the revolutionary octagon. First he built eight massive pillars of stone at each corner. Then, after combing England for trees of the right size, he finally settled for eight oaks weighing ten tons each and trimmed to 63 feet in length. These were to be the corner posts of the lantern.

The lantern tower itself, a construction of timber triangles, rises 60 feet and weighs a total of 400 tons. Such was the genius of Walsingham and his craftsmen that the entire structure rests on the stone pillars with a sheer perpendicular downward thrust. At the base of the octagon arches are the carved stone heads of those involved in its construction.

The Lady Chapel, completed in the mid-fourteenth century, sometime after the octagon, is the largest such chapel in England and its roof span of 46 feet gives it the

Below: The cathedral, looking east to west. The timber lantern rising from the ingenious central octagon is plainly visible.

Above: Rainwater is carried clear of the cathedral walls by grotesquely modelled gargoyles.
Above right: A detail from the stained glass window in the south transept.
Opposite: The view up into the great octagon amply demonstrates the skill of the medieval craftsmen who built it when the central tower collapsed in 1322.
Overleaf: Ely from the west front. The entrance is through the beautiful 13th century Galilee Porch.

widest medieval stone vault. Unhappily the Reformation destroyed much of the chapel's original charm: the stained glass windows were smashed and the sculpture and carvings ruined. However, what was spared is still worthy of attention, especially the arcade below the windows.

There is still a good deal of exquisite carving throughout the cathedral, particularly in the south-west transept. The Prior's Door, opening onto the cloisters from the nave, is a fine example of late Norman craftmanship while the fourteenth century choir stalls boast 62 superb misericords.

The west front entrance to Ely is through the lovely Galilee Porch dating from the thirteenth century. From here the entire length of the cathedral is impressively visible, along the narrow Norman nave with its nineteenth century roof paintings to the great stained glass window behind the presbytery and high altar at the east end.

Ely's oldest item is Ovin's Stone, the base of a cross and the only reminder that the cathedral has Saxon origins. The shrine of St Ethelreda contains the relics of Ely's foundress, a remarkable woman who was married to King Egfrid of Northumbria before becoming a nun and later Abbess of Ely.

Of the chantry chapels the most elaborate is Bishop Alcock's, the founder of Jesus College, Cambridge. Bishop West's chantry with its beautiful ceiling is also noteworthy. The finest of the monuments is that erected to the Earl of Worcester beheaded in the Wars of the Roses. It has a triple canopy and stands in the south choir aisle.

During the nineteenth century there was a great deal of restoration, both outside and inside the cathedral. Sir Gilbert Scott was in charge and apart from the insertion of some indifferent Victorian glass, did much to improve Ely's then fading glory.

Exeter

The interior of Exeter Cathedral is, without doubt, one of England's architectural glories. The richness and abundance of its stained glass and window tracery, the detailed woodwork and the decorative stonework is rarely equalled and virtually never excelled. The roof is the longest uninterrupted stretch of Gothic vaulting in the world: 300 feet of soaring stone supported on 30 moulded marble columns and looking not unlike some great avenue of stately trees.

The cathedral's exterior, while not matching the splendour inside, is still impressive. The west front with its niched statues of saints and monarchs is the most interesting although the depredations of age and weather have done much to reduce the overall effect.

Exeter's site dates back as far as 670 when it was used for a small monastery. This was replaced 200 years later by a minster which itself was destroyed by the Danes in 1003. King Canute rebuilt the minster in 1019 and in 1050 Leofric was enthroned as the See of Exeter's first Bishop. He died in 1072, bequeathing a famous set of books to the cathedral library.

Following the Norman Conquest, Exeter grew in importance and it was

Left: Exeter Cathedral, showing the exterior flying buttresses.

decided to extend and alter the existing buildings in keeping with the See's increasing influence. Work started in 1107 on what was to become a unique feature: two great transeptal towers – one on each side of the great structure instead of both in the centre – and in 1133 the new Norman edifice was consecrated. However, apart from the towers, little now remains from the Norman period.

The creation of the cathedral as we know it today was started in 1275 by Bishop Bronescombe. He built the Lady Chapel and the two adjacent chapels. His successor, Bishop Quivil, considerably enhanced the Lady Chapel and opened up the Norman towers, converting them into transepts with huge decorated windows. Thereafter each bishop who followed left his own distinctive impression, culminating with Bishop Grandisson who, among other achievements, completed the Gothic vaulting in the mid-fourteenth century.

Exeter suffered during the Reformation when a great deal of the decoration was either defaced or burnt. The seventeenth century Commonwealth Government added to the damage as did a series of devastating air raids in 1942. Thanks to devoted fund-raising and the dedication of craftsmen, Exeter is now restored – particularly on the inside – to its former magnificence.

As well as being a wonderful work of architecture, Exeter contains so many rare and exquisite treasures that it is impossible to list them all here. They include elaborately carved tombs, painted panels, a fourteenth century minstrel's gallery and a late fifteenth century clock which shows the earth at the centre of the dial with the sun and moon revolving around the outer circle.

Other outstanding features are the carved oak Bishop's Throne, completed in 1312 and standing 60 feet high, the Speke Chantry and the great east window, rebuilt in 1390 from the original of 1303.

Opposite: Looking east down Exeter's nave. It boasts the world's longest unbroken stretch of Gothic vaulting, 300 feet of grace and splendour.

Overleaf: Although Exeter's west front has worn considerably it still presents an impressive facade.

Below: A few of the innumerable niched statues once painted in brilliant colours, which line the west front.

Gloucester

In 1327 when Gloucester – then an abbey – seemed to be heading once more for bankruptcy, the monks accepted the body of the horribly murdered Edward II for burial. It had already been refused at Bristol and Malmesbury.

This hitherto rare display of financial acumen paid off. Once the funeral obsequies were over and Edward laid to rest, his tomb – and more importantly, Gloucester – became such a focus of pilgrimage that it was soon almost impossible to accommodate the crowds.

The abbey began deriving an enormous income from the pilgrims' offerings and it was not long before the money was put to good use – an extensive rebuilding programme. The rebuilding was carried out in the little known Perpendicular style making Gloucester, when it was finished, the birthplace of English Perpendicular Gothic architecture.

Work started in the transepts and choir. The old roof was removed, the east end apse pulled down and a vast perpendicular stone screen was taken up the inside of the Norman arcade, windows were inserted in the screen and a great lierne vault, 92 feet from the ground, erected over the whole. The apse was replaced with an immense stained glass window, 72 feet by 38 feet, the largest of its kind in the country. It dates from the mid-fourteenth century and commemorates those who fought at the Battle of Crécy in 1346.

Below: The fan vaulting in Gloucester's Great Cloister is unique in extent and complexity. Opposite: The cathedral from the east.

Opposite: Edward II's tomb is surmounted by this fine alabaster effigy. The tomb was erected by Edward III in memory of his murdered father.

Right: The reredos, or screen, behind the High Altar. It was designed by Sir Gilbert Scott in the 19th century.

In the centre of the presbytery, and overlooked by the Crecy Window, is the unusual tomb of Robert, Duke of Normandy, William the Conqueror's eldest son. His effigy, in wood, was made towards the end of the thirteenth century while the sarcophagus – also in wood – is fifteenth century. Robert died at Cardiff Castle in 1134 after being held a prisoner for 28 years by his brother, Henry I.

The beautiful canopied tomb of Edward II, with its forest of pinnacles and exquisite alabaster effigy, is to be found under the north arcade of the presbytery. It was erected by his son Edward III and is by far the most notable of the tombs in the cathedral.

It stands not too far from the Lady Chapel which was completed in 1499, marking the final flowering of Gloucester's perpendicular style. Almost the entire wall surface is filled with glass while its vaulted roof is supported on a series of graceful stone arches.

Gloucester's magnificent central tower was built in the mid-fifteenth century to replace one from the thirteenth century. It is 225 feet high and contains the only medieval great bell left in England.

On the north of the cathedral is the Great Cloister. Its fan-vaulting is believed to be unique, the first of such size and complexity built in England.

Hereford

Tradition has it that when King Ethelbert of East Anglia had his head struck off by Offa, King of Mercia in 794, his ghost demanded burial at Hereford. It is believed that a wooden church was erected over the tomb containing his body but this was succeeded in 825 by one of stone.

This in turn was replaced slightly more than two hundred years later and then, in 1056, it was burnt to the ground by Welsh and Irish raiders. In 1080 Robert de Lonsinga began the Norman restoration which was to continue until 1199 when the Early English style started to come to the fore. That in turn gave way to medieval or Decorated Gothic and finally, from the mid-fourteenth century, Perpendicular.

Hereford has had, therefore, a fairly complicated architectural history. This was aggravated by a questionable building programme undertaken by James Wyatt following the collapse of the west tower in 1786. This gave him the opportunity to destroy much of the original Norman work – especially in the nave – and resulted in a new and somewhat incongruous west front which between 1902 and 1908 was replaced with the present neo-Gothic facade.

None of this, however, detracts in any way from the impact of the splendidly dignified central tower. This, together with the now sadly lost Chapter House,

Opposite: Hereford Cathedral, looking towards the west front, sadly much damaged by Wyatt's programme of restoration during the 18th century.

Below: The cathedral library contains many treasures, including this exquisitely decorated Limoges enamel Becket reliquary dating from the 13th century.

Above: This crucifix which decorates the tomb of Peter Aquablanca (Bishop of Hereford from 1240 to 1268) is the only one to have survived the depredations of Cromwell's troops during the English Civil War.

Right: The chantry of John Stanbury, Bishop of Hereford from 1453 to 1474, is an exquisite example of decorative medieval architecture.

dates from the early fourteenth century and stands on the old Norman piers and arches. Until 1790 it had a lead-covered timber spire.

One of the cathedral's most beautiful interior features is the early thirteenth century Lady Chapel. Its five narrow lancet windows at the east end, set in elaborate frames, lend the chapel a special dignity. The reredos behind the altar was presented to Hereford in 1951: its panels, depicting the life of Mary, together with the separate figures of Ethelbert and St Cantelupe, Bishop of Hereford from 1275 to 1282, make it a worthy modern addition to an ancient setting.

Among Hereford's many treasures, probably the most unusual is the *Mappa Mundi*, which hangs in the north aisle of the choir. A unique late thirteenth century map of the world, it is drawn on vellum and shows Jerusalem at the centre. Close by is the Stanbury Tomb and Chantry. Stanbury, a Bishop of Hereford in the mid-fifteenth century was Henry VI's Confessor as well as being a distinguished architect having drawn up the plans for the chapel at Eton. His tomb and effigy is in alabaster while the chantry, opposite, is richly decorated.

There are nearly 1500 books in the cathedral's famous chained library situated off the cloisters. The books are chained to seventeenth century oak bookcases and it is the largest – and probably the finest – such library in the world. The oldest and most valuable book is the Anglo-Saxon Gospels, written in Latin during the last years of the eighth century. Also on display in the library is the thirteenth Beckett Reliquary in Limoges enamel.

Lichfield

Although Lichfield is one of England's smaller cathedrals its three magnificent and unique spires – the Ladies of the Vale – certainly make it one of the most distinctive. The central and tallest spire, rising to a height of 258 feet, was rebuilt in the second half of the seventeenth century after it had been destroyed by Cromwell's pitiless cannon. But the matching pair over the elaborate west front have survived since 1320.

The earliest cathedral at Lichfield was built in 700 to house the wooden shrine of St Chad, Bishop of Mercia from 669 to 672. Nothing, however, remains from those far off days neither does much from the first Norman building of 1140.

Lichfield as we know it today was built largely between 1195 and 1325 as a direct response to the crowds of pilgrims making their way to St Chad's Shrine. The old building proved too small to accommodate them and was pulled down. The earliest part of the new cathedral was the choir, built in the Early English style

Below: One of Lichfield Cathedral's most treasured possessions – St Chad's Gospel, an illuminated manuscript book written in the eighth century.

and restored in the nineteenth century by Sir Gilbert Scott. He installed the stalls and the equally ornate Bishop's Throne.

The nave was completed in 1258 and, apart from the roof, is unchanged. It is a particularly fine example of Early English architecture combined with that of the Decorated period.

At the far end of the nave is the exquisite Lady Chapel, built in the early fourteenth century. Its chief interest lies in seven of the nine stained glass windows at the apsidal east end. They are sixteenth century Flemish and were bought from Herckenrode Abbey, Belgium, in 1802.

As has already been stated, Cromwell's cannon gave Lichfield a terrible battering in the seventeenth century. The only part of the roof to survive was that over the thirteenth century Chapter House with its 13 canopied stalls. The upper part – the capital – of the central column was carved by four different craftsmen each of whom, as can be seen, indulged his own preference. The column carries on up into the second storey of the Chapter House known as the Treasury, but in fact used as the cathedral library.

The library contains Lichfield's greatest treasure: St Chad's Gospel, written and illuminated in the first years of the eighth century. It includes the complete Gospels of St Mark and St Matthew and is one of the finest manuscripts of its kind in Europe.

Lichfield's west front was extensively restored in the nineteenth century and unfortunately only five of the original thirteenth century statues are now left. These are situated in the north-west tower. All the rest are Victorian reproductions.

Right: The Lady Chapel with its fine display of 16th century Flemish stained glass.

Opposite: Lichfield Cathedral's richly decorated west front. It was restored extensively in the 19th century.

Lincoln

On April 15 1185 an unusual and totally unexpected earthquake shattered Lincoln's Norman cathedral buildings. All that was left standing were the two west towers and the west front. However, only seven years later rebuilding began and resulted in what is arguably Britain's finest cathedral.

The work started with the choir and the east transepts, continued with the main transepts, the chapter house, central tower and nave and finished with the cloisters, presbytery and retro-choir in the late thirteenth century.

This last – the retro-choir – is known as the Angel Choir and is Lincoln's main glory. It was built, surprisingly enough, by demolishing some of the first work at the east end of the cathedral. Whatever whim or architectural vagary dictated the decision, it left Lincoln – and the rest of the country – with the ultimate expression of English Gothic.

The Angel Choir houses an elaborate plinth on which a silver casket containing the head of St Hugh, the bishop who rebuilt Lincoln after the earthquake, used to stand. His coffin and shrine, once the object of pilgrims' veneration, has long since disappeared. There is some magnificent carving and sculpture, particularly the 30 angels between the shoulders of the ornate arches which line the triforium, or upper part of the wall, opening onto a gallery. The last shoulder on the north side contains a mischievous little figure known popularly as the 'Lincoln Imp'. He is shown emerging from a carving of foliage.

Another of Lincoln's fine features is its stained glass. The earliest is the great rose window, or Dean's Eye, at the north end of the great transept. It dates back to the early thirteenth century and has been longer in its setting than any other glass in the country. Opposite, at the other end of the transept is the Bishop's Eye. This bewilderingly complex display of medieval glass separated by flowing decorated tracery, was restored at the end of the eighteenth century.

It would take a week to see all the treasures of Lincoln, just as it would take a complete book to describe them. Everywhere you look there is a profusion of

Right: A 19th century stained glass window depicting scenes from the life of Moses.

Opposite: Lincoln's chief glory, the 13th-century Angel Choir.

wonderfully worked glass, stone and wood. The fourteenth century choir stalls and their superb misericords deserve special attention, as does the extraordinarily intricate pulpitum or choir screen.

Historically speaking the Chapter House is of especial interest. It was here in February 1301, while presiding over a Parliamentary session, that Edward I created his eldest son the Prince of Wales.

From the outside the west front is a splendid combination of the original Norman structure and Bishop Hugh's new building. There are the statues of 11 English kings above the central doorway while the turrets on either side of the front each has its own single statue: one is of Bishop Hugh and the other is the Swineherd of Stowe, a man who gave the cathedral every penny he possessed.

The two towers over the west front are 206 feet high while the central tower reaches 271 feet. It houses a five-and-a-half ton bell called 'Great Tom of Lincoln'. The central tower, rebuilt in the fourteenth century after the collapse of an earlier one, was once topped by a wooden spire. This gave it a total height of 524 feet, the highest in the country. However, it was wrecked by a storm in 1584 and never replaced.

Right: The west front.
Opposite: Lincoln Cathedral's central tower. Once topped by a wooden spire, it was never replaced after its collapse in 1584.
Overleaf: A few of the grotesque carved figures on the cathedral exterior.

Liverpool

Everything about Liverpool Cathedral is on the grand scale. From its mighty central tower to the incredible 9000 pipe organ, it is massive. This is the twentieth century's answer to the medieval builders: it was started in 1904 and when finished shortly, will be the world's largest cathedral after St Peter's in Rome.

The architect, Sir Giles Gilbert Scott – grandson of the renowned restorer of Gothic churches – was only 22 when he won the commission in competition with more than 100 aspirants. On July 19th 1904 Edward VII laid the foundation stone. Six years later the first part of the new cathedral, the Lady Chapel, was consecrated.

It is a very ornately decorated structure and differs from other Lady Chapels in that it projects from the south-east corner of the building, rather than extending directly behind the high altar. The stained glass windows commemorate various women, Biblical, historical and contemporary, while the screen behind the altar depicts the Nativity.

The First World War impeded progress but did not halt it entirely and the next part of the cathedral, the choir, eastern transepts and Chapter House, was consecrated in 1924.

Almost immediately afterwards the War Memorial Chapel and the Cenotaph were dedicated. The Cenotaph is made of richly carved wood and black fossil marble. It bears the Roll of Honour, an illuminated book now containing nearly forty thousand names. This is already regarded as one of Liverpool's most treasured possessions.

The work continued apace until being slowed by the Second World War

Left: Liverpool Cathedral's highly decorated and gilded High Altar. Its central feature is a study of the Last Supper.

Right: The main entrance to Liverpool Cathedral, through the Rankin Porch.

when the craftsmen and labourers dwindled away to a mere handful. In 1941 the central space under the tower and the west transepts were finished. Then, eight years later the central Vestey tower and the north and south porches reached completion. The tower is easily the cathedral's most dominant feature. It is 347 feet high and houses the heaviest peal of bells in the world. There are 14 altogether, 13 of which are grouped round the immense Bourdon – the bell with the lowest key – which weighs an incredible 14½ tons.

Another of the cathedral's unique features is the east window of the choir. It is the largest in the country, 76 feet by 44 feet, and takes the Te Deum as its theme. Under the window is the lavishly carved and gilded high altar, the reredos of which is actually a part of the wall itself – most unusual in cathedral architecture.

This is the first Gothic cathedral to have been built since the Reformation. It is an achievement that many thought impossible – the resurrection of the medieval ideal using modern skills and imagination.

Llandaff

The nave of Llandaff is dominated by a great concrete arch supporting an equally impressive cylindrical organ case. The sides of the case are decorated with 64 gilded pre-Raphaelite figures while the front provides the setting for Epstein's vast figure of Christ cast in unpolished aluminium. The whole concept is incredibly effective, not least because it is so unexpected in what is essentially a medieval church.

Despite this uncompromising concession to modernity, Llandaff has a history which stretches back further than any English cathedral. It was founded around 560 by Teilo, a missionary who took the name from a nearby river. Nothing now remains of the sixth century Christian outpost, nor does anything of a later church which stood on the site until the beginning of the twelfth century.

In 1120 a Norman bishop called Urban began building a new church, starting with the presbytery and choir. The dignified arch leading from behind the High

Left: The nave, dominated by the great aluminium statue of Christ by Epstein.

Right: Llandaff Cathedral from the south-east. Following the devastation caused by a German landmine in 1941 the building was more or less totally restored.

Altar to the Lady Chapel is a noteworthy survivor from this period. It is overlooked by a window designed by John Piper.

The Lady Chapel itself was built during the thirteenth century and has a particularly fine vaulted ceiling. It contains the tomb of William de Braose, bishop from 1266 to 1287.

Llandaff was sadly neglected after the Reformation and by the time Cromwell's soldiers used the nave as a beer house in the mid-seventeenth century, the cathedral was in a very sorry state. However, worse was to come. Storms in 1703 and 1723 brought down pinnacles, the south-west tower and the nave roof. Soon the once-proud building lay in virtual ruins.

A brave attempt at restoration was made in the second half of the eighteenth century but in doing so, much of the medieval structure was lost. Then, in 1835 a major restoration began and continued until 1869. During those 34 years the decaying cathedral regained much of its former dignity. The architect, a local man called John Pritchard, was responsible for some interesting innovations including, along the north and south walls of the nave, the sculpted heads of all the British monarchs from Richard III to Edward VIII. George VI and Elizabeth II were later added to the north side.

In January 1941 a German landmine undid the good work, its explosion causing more damage than had been achieved through storms, neglect and the Civil War. Llandaff was more or less sealed off – after Coventry the worst hit cathedral of the war.

But by August 1960, Llandaff was totally – and imaginatively – restored and its old features once more displayed. These include a Rosseti painting *The Seed of David* which forms a triptych in the Illtyd Chapel; the thirteenth century shrine of St Teilo and a series of Pre-Raphaelite porcelain panels in the Chapel of St Dyfig depicting the six days of the Creation.

Londonderry
St Columb's Church of Ireland Cathedral

During the famous siege of 1689 when Londonderry defended itself against the forces of King James II, a shell was fired into the cathedral yard. It was soon discovered that the shell contained the expected capitulation terms. A great cry of 'No surrender' split the air. Today, nearly three hundred years later, the words still mean the same but in a different context.

Overleaf: The interior of Londonderry's 17th century St Columb's Cathedral.

In 1913 the descendants of those who held the city erected a siege window in the vestibule. It depicts the relief of Londonderry after a siege lasting an incredible 105 days which had cost the lives of ten thousand of its citizens. The Chapter House, just off the vestibule, has an exhibition of various objects connected with the city's history, including the padlocks and keys of the gates which the celebrated apprentice boys locked in the face of the enemy.

St Columb's was built by the Irish Society in 1633 using what is now known as the 'Planters' Gothic' style of architecture. The spire was added at the beginning of the nineteenth century and then, towards the end of the century the cathedral was restored and extended. The roof rests on corbels, or stone projections, some of them representing earlier bishops of Londonderry.

Within the cathedral itself there are monuments to some of the seventeenth century 'Planters' – Scots and English immigrants sent over by James I to people Ireland's northern counties. The monument to Alexander Tomkins, an alderman, and his step-father John Elvin who became mayor, is particularly noteworthy.

There is some interesting glass – besides the seige window – including the St Columba window which depicts the saint on his sixth century mission to Britain and another dedicated to the memory of Mrs Frances Alexander, widow of a late nineteenth century bishop. Mrs Alexander is well remembered for her hymns, three of which are illustrated in the glass.

Left: An example of Planter's Gothic architecture, St Columb's Cathedral was built in 1663.

Manchester

A series of restorations, the last following an air raid in 1940, means that Manchester is now noted rather more for what it contains than for any architectural merit it might once have possessed. And, while it is true that the width of the nave is the greatest in the country – exceeding even York by ten feet – the cathedral's actual area is comparatively small.

Manchester was founded early in the fifteenth century when Henry V granted Thomas de la Warre permission to build a church alongside his existing priests' college. The original charter still hangs in the cathedral. Building began around 1422 and continued until 1522. When it was finished Manchester boasted – as it still does – some of the most magnificent wood carving to be found in any English cathedral.

The most obvious example is the screen dividing the nave from the choir. This screen – or pulpitum – is made of intricately worked solid oak, and has a fine display of painted panels. A new cornice was added in 1872 but it was designed to blend happily with its medieval setting.

Within the choir itself the stalls show early sixteenth century craftsmanship at its incomparable best. Each one of the 30 stalls is surmounted by an ornate canopy supported by elegant shafts. The misericords under the seats are also so cleverly detailed that it seems a pity they remain concealed.

When the fatal bomb fell in 1940 one of the worst hit casualities was the Lady Chapel. Amazingly, however, the screen separating it from the retro-choir was unscathed. This screen was made around 1440 and is the oldest in the cathedral. On the outside wall of the now restored Chapel is a gilded bronze statue of the Virgin and Child by the late Sir Charles Wheeler, one-time President of the Royal Academy. He has depicted her wearing the scarf, shawl and dress of a Lancashire mill girl.

Among the other interesting artistic pieces is a series of murals showing the Beatitudes in modern dress. They were painted by Carel Weight and fill the stone tracery over the double-arched entrance to the Chapter House.

Left: A contemporary picture of the extensive damage to Manchester Cathedral caused by an air raid in 1940.

Opposite: The nave with its elegant camber beam roof, tiled floor and unusually wide clerestroy windows.
Right: The main entrance to Manchester Cathedral.

Bottom right: An enchanting study of a farmer's wife chasing a fox which has made off with a goose forms part of a misericord in the choir stalls.
Below: An Anglo-Saxon stone carving of an angel. It was discovered when the north porch foundations were being dug in the late 19th century.

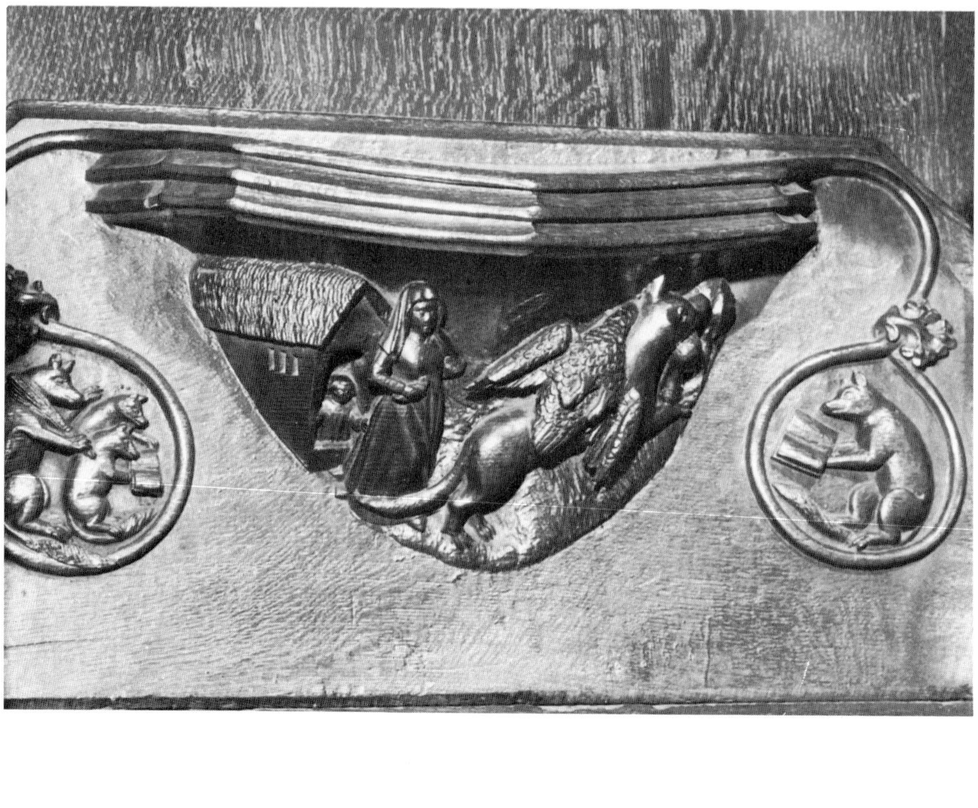

Norwich

The spire of Norwich Cathedral soars 315 feet – second only to Salisbury – while the tower from which it rises is not only the tallest Norman tower in the country but also one of the finest surviving from the Norman period. This, together with the splendidly elegant flying buttresses supporting the presbytery vault, are Norwich's most distinctive exterior features.

The architectural glory of the interior is undoubtedly the perfectly proportioned Norman apse at the cathedral's east end. The apse, or semi-circular cathedral end, is surmounted with a magnificent clerestory rebuilt in the fourteenth century after the original was destroyed when an earlier wooden spire collapsed.

Norwich Cathedral's foundation stone was laid in 1096 by Bishop Herbert de Losinga. By the time he died in 1119 he had completed the presbytery, the transepts, part of the central tower and the east end of the nave. In 1272 the citizens of Norwich rioted and set fire to the cathedral interior and burnt down most of the domestic buildings. The damage was so severe that six years later Norwich was re-consecrated.

Building continued throughout the thirteenth, fourteenth and early years of the fifteenth centuries. Norwich suffered considerably during the Civil War but quickly recovered after the Restoration.

Among the cathedral's various unique features is the fact that the cathedra, or

Right: A detail from a 14th century panel depicting the Ascension in the Ambulatory Chapel.

Opposite: Norwich Cathedral from the south side. The 14th century flying buttresses support the choir clerestory.

Right: The nave is 250 feet long and possesses a magnificent lierne vault built over the Norman walls in the 15th century.

Below: The south nave aisle. It dates mostly from the Norman period.

bishop's throne, is positioned east of the altar. This throne is Norwich's most treasured possession and dates back to the eighth century when the See of East Anglia was established at Dunwich. It is the oldest bishop's throne still used in England and incorporates pieces of stone from the ancient Saxon cathedral.

Norwich also contains what could well be England's oldest religious effigy: it is not certain whom it represents – possibly Losinga – but it is known to date back to around 1100 when it was placed in a niche above the north transept door. In 1968 it was moved into the ambulatory and placed near a seven sacrament fifteenth century font. The ambulatory's south walk leads to the fourteenth century Bauchon Chapel with its particularly fine and ornate bosses.

Other chapels contain exquisite wall panels painted by Norwich artists of the medieval era. The retable – frame of decorated panels at back of altar – in St Luke's is of special note. Just east of St Luke's Chapel is the last resting place of Edith Cavell, the British nurse executed by the Germans in 1915.

Away from the main body of the cathedral are the cloisters, the only two-storeyed monastic cloisters in England. They are also among the finest, with their window tracery and elaborately sculptured vault bosses.

Oxford

Oxford is unique for two reasons: it is the smallest cathedral in England and it is the only cathedral in the world which also serves as a college chapel – namely Christ Church.

It was originally founded as an eighth century nunnery and later rebuilt by the Normans. During the sixteenth century four of the eight nave bays were lost when Cardinal Wolsey wanted more space for the quadrangle of what was to be his Cardinal College. He also partly demolished the cloisters and used the stone – as well as that from the nave – to augment the materials he needed for the college. It is quite probable that had he not fallen from favour with Henry VIII, he would have eventually demolished the entire cathedral.

In 1546 Henry designated the by now much depleted building as cathedral of the new diocese of Oxford and instructed that it should also be used as the chapel of the newly founded Christ Church College.

The exterior, although interesting, is somewhat difficult to see. It is notable chiefly for the thirteenth century spire which is believed to be one of the oldest in the country.

The interior, however, is a delight, despite the fact that it dates from so many different periods. The intriguing double arches in the nave are undoubtedly Norman while the choir, with its exquisite fan vaulting is late fifteenth century. The roof of the nave is sixteenth century timber while that of the lantern is a hundred years earlier.

Left: Burne-Jones, the 19th century artist, designed several of Oxford's Christ Church Cathedral's stained glass windows. This shows a detail from the St Catherine Window.

Overleaf: Although the smallest of England's cathedrals, Christ Church qualifies as one of the most picturesque. The tip of the spire can be glimpsed above and behind the Great Hall.

There is some fine fourteenth and seventeenth century glass, the room itself being a magnificent example of thirteenth century architecture.

In the north aisle of the choir is the late thirteenth century leaf-sculpted base of what was once the shrine of St Frideswide, daughter of an eighth century king. An extremely rare fifteenth century wooden watching chamber is close by. St Frideswide's finely restored tomb now lies in the Lady Chapel.

Right: The 15th century pendant lierne vault.

Opposite: Christ Church Cathedral, Oxford, from the north.

Peterborough

Peterborough shares with Wells the distinction of an incomparable west front. It lacks the extravagant medieval sculpture of its Somerset counterpart but more than compensates by the sheer splendour of its architecture, the dominant feature being three 81 feet high ornate and deeply recessed arches.

The west front, a classic example of the early English design, is 156 feet wide and was built at the beginning of the thirteenth century, masking the earlier Norman facade. The central porch – a somewhat incongruous structure – was added in 1370.

Peterborough did not become a cathedral until the dissolution of the monasteries in the sixteenth century. Previously it was an abbey, with origins dating back to the seventh century. Following Viking raids in 870 when the abbey was burnt and its monks cruelly slaughtered, Peterborough lay in ruins for 100 years. It was eventually rebuilt by Aethelwold, Bishop of Winchester, who claimed he had been asked to do so in a dream. During the next century Peterborough was attacked again – this time by Hereward the Wake as a protest against the appointment of the first Norman bishop. Hereward's raid did not cause too much damage but an accidental fire in 1116 destroyed most of the abbey and its domestic buildings.

Two years later the Normans began to rebuild Peterborough. The work was to continue for 80 years finally resulting in much of what stands today. The nave with its wooden vault is particularly striking. The ceiling was painted around 1220 and is one of the most important pieces of medieval art in existence. It is decorated with saints, kings, monsters and bishops and is one of only four such ceilings left in Europe.

Just inside the west entrance, to the north of the door, is a late sixteenth

Below: Peterborough Cathedral's much restored 13th century west front. The porch was added in the following century.

Right: The interior of the central tower. Built originally by by the Normans it was replaced in the 14th and 19th centuries.

century portrait of Robert Scarlett the sexton who buried Catherine of Aragon and Mary, Queen of Scots. Catherine remains in the cathedral, commemorated by a tomb in the north aisle of the presbytery. Mary's tomb, however, was removed by her son James I in 1612 to a more magnificent setting in Westminster Abbey. The site of her original tomb at Peterborough is marked with a simple stone tablet fixed to a column on the south side of the presbytery.

By the fourteenth century the central tower – like so many Norman towers – had become unsafe. It was taken down and replaced with a lower one, itself rebuilt in 1884. Many of the old materials were used and the result, especially from inside, is pleasing. The wooden vaulted ceiling is painted and decorated. The ceiling of the choir is also richly decorated although many of its fittings – including the stalls and bishop's throne – date from the late nineteenth century.

Following the destruction of the Civil War Peterborough remained in a fairly indifferent state until the early years of the nineteenth century when an extensive programme of restoration was started. A great deal of new Gothic stonework went into the cathedral and the presbytery's fifteenth century painted wooden vault now looks down on stalls and box pews from a much later period.

Right: The south transept. A subway running underneath gives access to the foundations of the 10th century Saxon church.

Ripon

The crypt at Ripon has survived since the seventh century, one of the few Anglo-Saxon ecclesiastical buildings still extant. It is a small cramped place, reached by a stair from the nave. On the north side of the crypt is a narrow hole known as Wilfred's Needle, once used as a test of chastity. Only those slim enough to squeeze through into the passage outside were adjudged pure.

Ninth century Danish raiders reduced the church above the crypt to a ruin but it was rebuilt the following century and declared a place of sanctuary. But any criminal who claimed the right of shelter at Ripon soon found himself before a church court and subsequent trial by ordeal.

The Norman Conquest saw Ripon once more in ruins and it remained so until 1080 when Thomas of Bayeux, Archbishop of York began to rebuild. The vaulted undercroft beneath the Chapter House – now a mortuary chapel – remains from this period as does the apsidal east end of the Chapter House itself.

Ripon as we know it today dates from 1154 and the arrival at York of Archbishop Roger Pont l'Eveque. During the 27 years before his death he built Ripon into what is now a classic example of the Transitional Norman style.

His successors continued the work, notably Walter de Grey, who contributed the somewhat severe west front with its twin towers. These were originally topped with wooden spires sheathed in lead but they were removed in 1664 as four years earlier the spire of the central tower had collapsed for the second time.

The much restored rather squat central tower now provides – internally – one of Ripon's outstanding architectural features: it has two round and two pointed arches, a direct result of the fifteenth century builders' failure to finish remodelling the tower. They managed to complete the two on the south and east sides in the pointed Perpendicular style but left those on the north and west as round twelfth century Norman Transitional.

Other features include the beautiful canopied fifteenth century choir stalls, the stone bosses in the choir ceiling and the remarkable twentieth century reredos, a memorial to the men of Ripon who died in the First World War.

Left: The 15th century canopied choir stalls, among Ripon Cathedral's most interesting and attractive features. The central organ case was designed by Sir Gilbert Scott in 1860.

Overleaf: The squat towers of Ripon tend to make the cathedral look rather lower than its actual height.

Rochester

The ancient Saxon cathedral at Rochester had served the community for over four hundred years before a new Norman bishop was installed in 1077. Bishop Gundulph, seeing the neglected condition of the cathedral, decided to rebuild it to his own plans.

Gundulph's first priority was a 50 feet high, massively strong, stone tower. As the architect of London's White Tower and Rochester Castle, Gundulph was well-versed in military matters and it is presumed he intended that the tower should be used for defensive purposes – should the need arise. It still stands situated rather incongruously between the two transepts on the north side of the cathedral.

Building on the cathedral proper began in 1080, starting with a raised choir and presbytery at the eastern end. Gundulph died before his work was done but his splendid nine-bay nave – although incomplete – must have seemed a worthy monument. Two later bishops finished the nave and considerably extended the

Below: A complete view of Rochester Cathedral, looking down on it from the west.

Opposite: Rochester's central tower was first built in 1343. Since then it has collapsed and been rebuilt several times, the latest as recently as 1904.

west front. Much of Gundulph's earlier work was re-cased with better stone, imported from Caen.

The west front door was built in the mid-twelfth century and is considered one of the finest in England. With its elaborate sculptured tympanum – semi-circular stonework over a door or window – and its receding arches, the door is probably Rochester's most outstanding feature. The much-weathered statues of Henry I and Queen Matilda positioned on either side of the door are reputed to be the earliest such statues still in existence.

In 1179 most of the city of Rochester was levelled by fire – the second since 1137 – and the cathedral was badly damaged. Fortunately the nave arcades and the walls of the choir survived. The east wall in the cloister garth still bears a faint red tinge.

Building and rebuilding continued well into the fifteenth century when the great perpendicular window was inserted in the west front. It was renewed in the nineteenth century and now serves as a memorial to the Royal Engineers who perished in the Afghan and South African wars.

There was some unsympathetic restoration carried out in the nineteenth century but, by and large, Rochester remains a reasonable example of one of the Norman's smaller cathedrals. It contains the usual tombs to successive bishops as well as several interesting wall paintings, including the thirteenth century Wheel of Fortune standing opposite the Bishop's throne in the choir. Among the older parts of the cathedral, the best surviving piece of craftsmanship from the fourteenth century is the beautifully carved and decorated doorway from the south choir transept to the Chapter Room.

Right: The west door demonstrates the skill of Norman craftsmen at their best. It is thought to be one of the finest of its kind in England.

St Albans

St Albans was founded as a Benedictine abbey in 793 to commemorate a Roman soldier who, when he was beheaded nearly 500 years earlier for harbouring a priest, became Britain's first Christian martyr.

The abbey was built on the site where he died, the crown of a hill overlooking the ancient town of Verulamium – now better known as St Albans. By 1088 the first Norman abbot, Paul of Caen, had rebuilt the Saxon abbey using bricks from the ruined Roman town. It was re-dedicated in 1115 and then rebuilt and extended again from 1200 until the year before Magna Carta, when St Albans had become the country's richest monastic house.

Henry VIII proposed that St Albans should become a cathedral when he dissolved the monasteries. The townspeople, however, preferred to retain it as a parish church. As such it was far too large and fell into disrepair until 1856 when Sir Gilbert Scott was commissioned to begin a restoration. Then, in 1877, it was created the cathedral of the new diocese of St Albans.

From the exterior there is little to commend St Albans except perhaps the Norman tower. Inside, however, the nave – the longest medieval nave in existence, 257½ feet – does have a certain majesty.

Right: St Albans from the west front. Along with much of the rest of the cathedral the west front was completely rebuilt in the late 19th century by Lord Grimthorpe, a wealthy and somewhat forceful benefactor. He insisted that the restoration be carried out to his own specifications, with not always pleasing results.

Opposite: The decorated wooden vault over the choir was erected in the 13th century and painted with its eagle and lamb motif two centuries later. The reredos beneath dates from 1484; it was restored around 1900.

Above: St Albans possesses some fine 13th and 14th century wall paintings. Until fairly recently they were hidden by whitewash. This particular study, of Christ on the Cross, was cleaned in 1955.
Above right: The shrine of St Alban. Behind is the early 15th century watching chamber from which monks kept a wary eye on pilgrims at the shrine.

It contains the remains of thirteenth and fourteenth century wall paintings on west and south sides of the Norman piers. There are also some fine painted panels on the choir ceiling; they have lasted unscathed since the fifteenth century despite once being plastered over. The choir is separated from the nave by a fourteenth century stone rood screen – the only screen of its type in an English cathedral.

The presbytery has a unique wooden vault which was painted in 1450 and is dominated by the vast and incredibly ornate reredos behind the altar. It was erected in the late fifteenth century and extensively restored in the early 1900s. To the east of the presbytery, and behind the high altar, is St Alban's Chapel. This houses the saint's shrine, the base of which was re-assembled in 1872 from about two thousand fragments of the original pedestal found among the rubble of a wall which blocked the arches at the east end of the chapel. On the north side of the chapel is the wooden watching chamber where monks guarded the shrine from over-eager pilgrims. The back of the chamber has delightful carvings of scenes from rural life.

On the south side stands the magnificent thirteenth century tomb of Humphrey, Duke of Gloucester and Henry V's brother. Richly decorated with statuettes, it is covered by a lofty canopy and protected by a wrought-iron Sussex grille.

The Lady Chapel at the east end of the cathedral was completed in the fourteenth century. It was freely restored in the nineteenth century although it still displays its elaborate window tracery and niched effigies.

St Asaph's

St Asaph is the smallest ancient cathedral in England and Wales. However, this has not prevented it from suffering the same misfortunes as the majority of larger British cathedrals.

It was founded as far back as 560 by the missionary St Kentigern after he had been exiled from Scotland. He was succeeded by St Asaph as bishop. The original building was rebuilt by the Normans and then destroyed by the English in the thirteenth century. In the next century it was a Welshman, the warrior Prince Owain Glyndwr who laid it waste.

In 1482 St Asaph was rebuilt yet again and managed to survive until the Civil War when, once more, it suffered considerable damage. In 1714 a fierce storm put paid to the roof and 65 years later the Chapter House was pulled down. The cathedral then lay in ruins until the nineteenth century when it was painstakingly and extensively restored by Sir Gilbert Scott.

The library, or museum, contains several interesting and rare books including the first Welsh translation of the Bible accomplished by Bishop William Morgan in 1588. There is also a display of some fine pieces of sixteenth and seventeenth century silver.

Overleaf: A general view of St Asaph, the smallest cathedral in England and Wales.

Below: The somewhat austere but dignified interior of St Asaph.

St David's

St David's, unlike most other cathedrals, does not dominate its surroundings. Instead it nestles in a hollow, its tranquil sandstone peacefully harmonizing with the backcloth of fields and coastal hills.

This is the oldest cathedral settlement in Britain. It has a continuous history dating back to the mid-sixth century when it served as a remote Welsh outpost of the Christian faith. The founder was Dewi Sant – St David, the patron saint of Wales. He forged such a feeling of religious community and extended the influence of his church so far, that it lasted as a pilgrim centre centuries after his death.

William the Conqueror visited St David's in 1081 but it was not until 1115 that the monks were forced to accept a royal nominee as their bishop. He was called Bernard and, once he had re-organized the monastery's working structure, he started re-building and re-modelling on a modest scale. In 1131 St David's was consecrated. Forty years later Henry II made a pilgrimage there as part of his atonement for Becket's murder by which time St David's income was large enough for the start of three centuries of building.

From the outside the cathedral is conventional enough – if not to say austere –

Left: The restored front of St Davids, with the adjacent medieval chapel.

Opposite: The nave of St Davids contains a mixture of styles and age ranging from the carved oak 16th century roof to the 20th century organ.
Overleaf: The Bishop's Throne. It is graced with three intricate canopies and dates from the early 16th century.

but this belies the magnificence of the interior. The most immediate and probably the most striking feature is the unique sixteenth century carved Irish oak ceiling. It is profusely and elaborately ornamented, the richness of the decoration contrasting beautifully with the plain unpainted wood surface.

The roof of the presbytery is also splendidly decorated, but in warm glowing colours handpainted in the fourteenth century. It looks down on the somewhat awkwardly placed white stone tomb of Edmund Tudor, the Earl of Richmond. Standing in the centre of the tiled presbytery floor, the tomb is separated from the High Altar by a low rail. Tudor's remains were transferred from the dissolved church of Grey Friars at Carmarthen, on the instructions of his grandson, Henry VIII.

Another interesting feature linking St David's with the monarchy is the medieval royal stall, the only such stall in a British cathedral. It was used by Elizabeth II in 1955; before this however, the last royal visitor to St David's was Edward I in 1284.

There are some particularly fine and fascinating fifteenth century misericords in the choir stalls and the Bishop's Throne – a century younger – has three elaborately pinnacled canopies. The simple shrine to St David himself stands in the north aisle of the choir; his relics, discovered in a rubble-filled recess during mid-nineteenth century restoration work, are contained in an oak casket in the Chapel of the Holy Trinity.

Below: St Davids has never intruded on its surroundings. Instead it nestles modestly in a hollow, blending peacefully with the Welsh landscape.

During the seventeenth and eighteenth centuries St David's, despite valiant efforts, decayed. The eminent architect John Nash attempted a restoration at the end of the eighteenth century but the results were surprisingly tasteless. It was left to the great Victorian Sir Gilbert Scott to rectify the error.

St Paul's

Although the mighty dome of St Paul's Cathedral surmounted by its gold cross has long ago been dwarfed by twentieth century office blocks, it still remains one of London's most famous landmarks and a lasting tribute to the architect, Sir Christopher Wren.

St Paul's stands on the site of four previous cathedrals bearing the same name. The first was built in the seventh century and destroyed by fire; the second was wrecked by the Vikings; the third suffered a fire and the fourth, built byBishop Maurice, chaplain to William the Conqueror, was destroyed by yet another fire – the Great Fire of London in 1666. All that was left of the medieval cathedral – the largest church in England – was a few columns, part of the walls and a strange shrouded effigy of John Donne, Dean of St Paul's from 1621 until his death in 1631.

Sir Christopher Wren had already been involved in early plans for the restoration of the Norman cathedral. Now he was asked to submit plans for a totally new building. Wren produced three schemes: the first was rejected as untraditional; the second – the magnificent oak model of which can be seen in the trophy room – was turned down for the same reason but eventually the third was grumblingly accepted, with reservations by the Commissioners.

The foundation stone was laid on June 21st 1675 and the cathedral finally completed in 1708. The whole project had been so beset with argument and controversy that it was three years later before Wren received payment in full – and then only after he had personally petitioned Queen Anne. He was dismissed as Surveyor General in 1718 and died in 1723 at the age of ninety one. His body was buried in the crypt – the largest in Europe – and his tomb marked with the

Overleaf: When the soot and grime was cleaned away in the mid-1960s, St Paul's white Portland stone was revealed again after 250 years.

Left: The incomparable west front of St Paul's Cathedral, one of London's most famous and best-loved landmarks.

Opposite: The pre-Raphaelite painter Holman Hunt's famous Light of the World. It hangs in the south aisle of the nave. Hunt himself is buried in the crypt, the largest in Europe.

word's 'Si monumentum requiris, circumspice' – 'If you seek his monument, look round'.

Wren shares the crypt with many of Britain's most illustrious names. Only two, however, the Duke of Wellington and Lord Nelson, are actually interred in their tombs: the others were laid to rest in the ground. These include the painters Holman Hunt, Reynolds, Turner and Millais, and the composer, Sir Arthur Sullivan. Wellington is also commemorated by a massive monument, which took 20 years to build, situated in the north aisle of the nave.

The stunningly beautiful interior of St Paul's was decorated by some of the world's leading seventeenth and eighteenth century craftsmen: Grinling Gibbons carved the choir stalls; Jean Tijou made the exquisitely complex wrought-iron sanctuary gates; while the eight frescoes in the dome were painted by James Thornhill, who was knighted in the year 1720 and also appointed serjeant painter to the Crown.

The dome is St Paul's crowning glory, both inside and out. It is 102 feet in diameter and reaches 364 feet into the air at the tip of its cross – just 40 feet lower than the spire at Salisbury. It survived the bombs of the Second World War although the choir roof and the north transept suffered direct hits. Much of the stained glass was so badly damaged during this period that it was later replaced with the clear glass of today. This was what Wren had intended originally and from the way the light enhances the interior, it is easy to see why.

In the mid 1960s St Paul's Portland stone was cleaned. The removal of two and a half centuries of soot and grime revealed once more the quality and soft whitish colour of the cathedral fabric as well as exposing some hitherto barely discernible carving.

Right: The interior of the great dome is decorated with 18th century frescoes by James Thornhill, later to become serjeant-painter to the Crown.

Salisbury

As well as being one of England's loveliest cathedrals Salisbury is, architecturally, one of the most important. Built between 1220 and 1284 it is the only example of a medieval cathedral which is wholly consistent in both design and construction. True, its lofty spire – 404 feet high and the tallest in the country – was not added until the mid-fourteenth century, but its tapering delicacy complements perfectly the elegant proportions of the main building below.

Salisbury possesses probably the most attractive setting of Britain's cathedrals. It is approached across the stately eighteenth century lawns of the close, entered through three medieval gates. The close itself, walled in 1333, contains several buildings which pre-date the completion of the cathedral. These include the Bishop's Palace, now the Cathedral School. The most notable of the other later houses is Mompesson House, built by a wealthy merchant family in 1701 and still containing much of the original plasterwork and panelling.

The first cathedral was sited at Old Sarum, a hill-fort town. Five days after it was consecrated in 1092 lightning so severely damaged the structure that it had to be rebuilt. However, it was not long before Bishop Richard Poore, frustrated by lack of a proper water supply, the incessant howling of the wind, the harrassment of his congregations by insensitive soldiers and the continuing complaints of rheumatism by his clergy, petitioned the Pope for permission to erect a new

Below: The nave is 230 feet long and 81 feet high. Everything in it dates from the 13th century.

Right: Salisbury Cathedral viewed across its stately lawns, from the south-west.

cathedral elsewhere. This was duly granted and in 1220, on a well-watered flat site two miles south, work began.

The first section to be finished was the Trinity Chapel at the east end. It was consecrated in 1225 and a plain black stone slab now marks the position of the old shrine of St Osmund, the bishop who completed the first cathedral at Old Sarum. The chapel also contains several tombs, the most notable of which is the imposing monument to the Earl of Hertford and his wife, Lady Jane Grey. A further feature of the chapel, the roof of which is supported by two rows of slender black Purbeck marble columns, is the thirteenth, fourteenth and sixteenth century glass.

By 1258 the nave, transepts and choir were virtually finished and Salisbury was consecrated. The bishop at the time was Giles de Bridport and a handsomely-sculptured tomb – carved with scenes from his life – was later erected for him in the south choir aisle. The cloisters, the largest and earliest of any English cathedral, were completed by 1270, one of their purposes being to provide a passage – the

Right: Salisbury's west front was completed in the mid-13th century. However, many of the larger statues are Victorian additions and do little to enhance the facade.

Plumberies – between the cathedral and the octagonal Chapter House, built between 1263 and 1284. Cromwell's soldiers caused considerable damage to the Chapter House but it was restored in the nineteenth century. Its beautifully fan-vaulted roof rises from a single slender central pillar. The sides are lined with stone seats, above which runs a frieze of thirteenth century stone bas-reliefs depicting Old Testament stories.

There is much to see throughout the cathedral, including many elaborate tombs and monuments. An item of particular fascination is the fourteenth century clock mechanism at the west end of the north aisle. This mechanism – which still works – is believed to be the oldest in Europe. It was installed originally in the old detached bell tower, pulled down in 1790. The fifteenth century library, over the east side of the cloisters, contains many rare and ancient treasures. The most outstanding is one of the four original copies of Magna Carta and a tenth century Gallican Psalter.

Left: The Audley Chantry, built to commemorate Bishop Edward Audley who died in 1524.

Overleaf: The 13th century chapter house with its delicately beautiful fan vault supported by one slender pillar.

Southwark

Towards the end of the nineteenth century Southwark had deteriorated to such an extent that demolition seemed almost inevitable. However, in 1890 London's South Bank cathedral – then a parish church – was reprieved and totally restored. Today, although crowded by other buildings, it remains second only to Westminster in its Gothic glory.

In the days of Edward the Confessor a monastery stood on the site but in 1106 it was reconstructed and 64 years later rededicated to Thomas Becket, following his untimely death at Canterbury. In the early years of the thirteenth century the church was devastated by a fire. The repairs took nearly 100 years and then, in 1385, there was another fire. Southwark was restored again in the fifteenth century and became a parish church in 1539 when Henry VIII dissolved the monasteries. During the eighteenth century decay set in, gradually worsening until the restoration of 1890.

There are still traces of the early building to be found in the interior, even though the nave itself has been completely rebuilt. Sections of thirteenth century arcading can be seen in the south-west corner while at the west end some fine

Right: The tomb of John Gower, Poet Laureate to both Richard II and his successor, Henry IV. Gower, who died in 1408, reclines on three of the books which he wrote.

Left: Southwark Cathedral was saved from demolition in 1890 and painstakingly restored to its present state.

carved bosses have survived from the fifteenth century wooden roof. An even earlier remnant is a twelfth century door situated in the north aisle which once led to the long disappeared cloisters.

The choir and retro-choir are classic examples of Early English architecture and, generally speaking, Southwark's strongest features; the ornate sixteenth century altar screen is also worth attention. Its Tudor statues have gone but the twentieth century restoration has been sensitively carried out. The aisles of the choir contain several fine tombs including one for James I's 'gentleman porter' John Trehearne and another for Richard Humble, a seventeenth century alderman.

On the east side of the north transept is the Harvard Chapel, dedicated to John Harvard, founder of the famous American university. He was baptized at Southwark in 1607 and emigrated in 1638. The chapel also contains a tablet commemorating the play and song writer, Oscar Hammerstein, who died in 1960.

Southwell Minster

Opposite: Southwell's twin-towered west front.

There is probably no other cathedral in Britain where medieval stone carving reaches such a peak of artistic perfection as it does at Southwell. Nowhere is this more evident than in the chapter house, built at the end of the thirteenth century and Southwell's most celebrated feature.

The entrance to this exquisite octagonal chamber from the vestibule is through a particularly beautiful arched doorway, divided by a slender pillar of extreme delicacy. The equally delicate shafts on each side of the arch provide rare examples of thirteenth century marble. The tops of these shafts and two of the arch mouldings are decorated with stone leaves, intricately and lovingly carved.

Inside the chapter house itself, the most immediately noticeable impression is the lack of a central pillar. This is because the chamber is unusually small – only 31 feet in diameter – and consequently there is no need for an additional support under the magnificent star-vaulted roof. The central boss in the roof is – like every boss on the arched ribs – carved with leaves. The foliage theme predominates: the canopies above each of the 36 stalls and the capitals being decorated with numerous and easily identified foliage, including oak, vine, maple and hawthorn.

Although the chapter house is deservedly the high-point of Southwell's attractions, the cathedral still possesses certain other interesting features. One of these is the fourteenth century stone screen which separates the choir from the nave. This is richly decorated with more than two hundred sculpted heads and figures, including caricatures of the craftsmen actually engaged in its creation. The

Right: The chapter house star vault with its delicately carved rib bosses.

Right: The entrance to the chapter house features some of the finest medieval stone carving in Britain.

canopies of the attached stalls are carved with the ubiquitous leaves. The brass lectern in the choir, fashioned in the shape of an eagle around 1500 was rescued from a lake where it had been thrown by the monks of nearby Newstead Abbey following the Dissolution. It eventually ended up in the hands of a Nottingham dealer from whom it was bought and presented to Southwell in 1805.

From the north transept, steps lead down into what was once the transept's east wall apse. Since the First World War it has served as the Airmen's Chapel. The altar cross and other fittings were made from the parts of an aircraft which crashed over France.

The origins of Southwell date back to the mid-tenth century when a church was established by Oskytel, Archbishop of York. Hardly anything remains of the Anglo-Saxon building except some pavement fragments in the south transept and a carved tympanum now serving as a lintel over a door in the west wall of the north transept.

The rebuilding of Southwell began during the Norman period with the nave, transepts and west front towers and continued until the end of the thirteenth century. It suffered the indignity of being used as a stable for Parliamentarian horses in the mid-seventeenth century and much of the sculpture and stained glass was smashed beyond repair. Restoration work was carried out in both the eighteenth and nineteenth centuries.

Wells

The west front of Wells Cathedral is a Gothic masterpiece and universally recognized as the most exquisite among Britain's cathedrals. It serves as a screen for an incredible display of statues – once numbering four hundred but now reduced to three hundred – half of which are life-size or larger.

This is undoubtedly the finest collection of medieval statues in the country. Running in six tiers they represent monarchs, prophets, apostles, saints and angels although many have suffered badly from the depredations of age, weather and vandalism. Their bright colours have long since faded but when newly finished by local craftsmen in 1249 they must have seemed one of the wonders of the medieval age.

Wells, often described as our most 'poetic' cathedral, was consecrated in 1239 and the building finally completed in the mid-fifteenth century. The great central tower was raised between 1315 and 1322. This increased the weight so much that sixteen years later cracks started appearing in the masonry and the tower began tilting westwards.

The solution to what could have been a disaster, took the form of ingenious inverted arches designed to transfer the load from west to east; widening the foundations and bracing the tower supports. The arches, inserted around 1338 on three sides – the choir screen providing the necessary support on the fourth – now

Left: The nave, showing one of the three great 'scissor' arches erected under the central tower in 1338 to act as extra support for the newly heightened central tower which, it was feared, might prove too heavy for the foundations.

Above: An impressive example of fan vaulting .
Opposite: The west front, one of the most outstanding examples of 13th century architecture still in existence today.
Overleaf: Wells Cathedral contains some very fine stained glass, especially at the east end.

form one of the cathedral's most interesting and striking features. Needless to say the tower has remained solid and upright ever since.

Another feature is the early fourteenth century elevated Chapter House, octagonal in shape and so beautifully decorated that it is surely one of the finest from this period. The worn stairway to the Chapter House was extended to the Chain Gate – a covered way from the cathedral to the Vicar's Hall – in the mid-fifteenth century.

The Lady Chapel, built around the same time, is also a classic example of medieval architecture and craftsmanship at its best. The chapel is linked to the stone-panelled presbytery by a splendidly vaulted retro-choir and possesses five large stained glass windows of which only one is not early fourteenth century, although they have all been patched at later dates. Wells' finest piece of stained glass is the Golden Window inserted in 1340 on the east side of the presbytery.

The cathedral contains the usual tombs of bishops and four fifteenth century chantry chapels of which one, Bishop Beckington's, retains its medieval colouring The Victorian choir stalls incorporate about 60 misericords dating from the early fourteenth century.

Outside the cathedral itself is the moated Bishop's Palace where swans pull a bell rope when they want to be fed and the unique Vicar's Close, two rows of 21 houses built in the mid-fourteenth century.

Westminster Abbey

Strictly speaking, as Westminster Abbey – not to be confused with the neo-Byzantine Roman Catholic cathedral nearby – only enjoyed cathedral status between 1540 and 1550 it has no place in this book. However, its unique situation as Britain's 'royal' church and all the concomitant splendour more than ensures its deserved inclusion.

Westminster was built first by the saintly English king, Edward the Confessor and consecrated on December 28th 1065, a few days before his death. On Christmas Day the following year the victorious William the Conqueror staged his coronation in the abbey. Since then, except for Richard I, Edward V and Edward VIII, every English monarch has been crowned there. On each occasion the ancient coronation chair, made in 1300 to house the Stone of Scone – captured from the Scots in 1296 – is brought out of St Edward's Chapel.

Many of them are also buried at Westminster, sharing their last resting place with great men and women from almost every walk of life: statesmen, authors, poets, musicians, scientists and fighting men. The eighteenth century saw the erection of memorials to eminent people buried elsewhere.

In 1245, less than two hundred years after Edward's great abbey was completed, Henry III pulled it down and started again. He wanted it refashioned in the French style – full of light and gracefully proportioned. In 1268 the remains of the now canonized Edward were brought back to Westminster from their

Below: Henry VII's ornate and elaborate 16th century chapel is probably Westminster's chief glory.

Overleaf: Eleanor of Castille, wife of Edward I, rests in a tomb in St Edward's Chapel. She died in 1290, 17 years before her husband.
Opposite: The west front of Westminster Abbey, Britain's royal church.

temporary home and enshrined in a tomb of such magnificence that it virtually bankrupted Henry III. Part of it was destroyed in 1540 following the dissolution of the monasteries but later restored during the reign of Mary I. Close by are the tombs of several other kings and queens, including Henry III himself.

Building continued slowly after Henry III's death in 1272 and it was not until the end of the fourteenth century that the abbey was largely complete. Then, in 1503, Henry VII decided he wanted a new Lady Chapel. The next 16 or so years were spent creating Henry VII's Chapel, certainly the chief glory of Westminster and one of the finest of its kind anywhere in the world. Henry VII and his queen lie in a vast Italianate tomb, surrounded by innumerable statues and looked down on by a fan vaulted roof of breathtaking beauty. Close by are the tombs of Mary, Queen of Scots and Elizabeth I while the banners lining the walls belong to the Knights Grand Cross of the Order of the Bath. The chapel has been theirs since 1725.

Those who died anonymously during the First World War are commemorated by a black slab of moving simplicity, the tomb of the Unknown Warrior, set in the floor near the west entrance. Beneath the stone lie the remains of an unknown soldier brought back from France and buried with great pomp on Armistice Day, November 11, 1920. Nearer the west door is another memorial, this time to Sir Winston Churchill, unveiled by the Queen in 1965.

Apart from general restoration and routine maintenance, no major building has occurred since 1734 with the completion of the west front towers. Until then these were only half-built, giving the abbey an unfinished air. They were finally brought to their present height by the architect Nicholas Hawksmoor, using an original design of Sir Christopher Wren.

Above: One of Westminster's treasures, a gilded plate used for the collection of alms or donations for the poor and needy.
Right: A portrait of St Peter, part of a 13th century retable.

Westminster Cathedral

Twelve and a half million bricks went into building Westminster Cathedral, England's leading Roman Catholic church, and it was constructed in the remarkably short time of eight years, from 1895 to 1903.

From outside it is quite unlike any other church, the red bricks alternating with greyish-white limestone in narrow bands to give it an exotic neo-Byzantine air. Its campanile – or bell tower – is square and reaches 284 feet to the top of the cross.

The cathedral interior is truly vast, 342 feet long and 149 feet wide and is laid out in the basilican pattern with four domes in the roof. At the west end are two huge columns made from red Norwegian granite. At the moment the decoration is incomplete but when finished it is intended that the walls and piers will be covered with coloured marble up to a height of 30 feet. Beyond that the walls – and the insides of the domes – will be lined with mosaics.

The side chapels, however, are already richly decorated. One of the most splendid is the Chapel of the Blessed Sacrament on the left of the Sanctuary. Its sumptuous mosaics symbolizing the Trinity and the Blessed Sacrament were fashioned between 1956 and 1962 by Boris Anrep.

Other chapels include the Chapel of St Patrick and the Saints of Ireland. This acts as a memorial to all the Irishmen who died in the First World War, each regiment being commemorated with a marble tablet. Next door is the chapel dedicated to St Andrew and the Saints of Scotland. This is decorated in a typically Byzantine manner and contains a set of impressive choir stalls made from inlaid ebony.

The altar table in the Sanctuary consists of a great block of Cornish granite

Left: The Lady Chapel.

Above: Westminster Cathedral's striking and unusual exterior.

weighing 12 tons. It is flanked with coloured marble arcades while the baldacchino, or canopy, above is made of white marble supported by columns of yellow Verona marble.

An early fifteenth century Madonna in alabaster can be found in the south transept while above on the pier there is an interesting bronze panel by Giacomo Manzu depicting St Teresa of Lisieux.

The crypt under the main body of the cathedral contains several relic chambers. One holds a mitre which once belonged to Thomas Becket, another, fragments of the True Cross.

Winchester

The origins of Winchester Cathedral date back as far as 645 although apart from the mortuary chests containing the bones of various Anglo-Saxon monarchs – including Canute and his wife Emma – nothing now remains from those days when Winchester was the capital of England.

The old cathedral was enlarged in the tenth century but as usual it was the Normans who were responsible for the basis of what stands today. In 1079 Bishop Walkelyn, successor to the last Anglo-Saxon bishop, started building the nave, transepts, choir and chapel, finishing in 1093 when the new cathedral was consecrated. Slightly more than a century later the Norman eastern chapel was pulled down and replaced with a retro-choir and a Lady Chapel, flanked by two other chapels.

This provided a more suitable setting for St Swithin's shrine. Swithin, an earlier bishop, died in 862 leaving instructions that he was to be buried *outside* the old cathedral. When it was decided in 971 to transfer his remains to the interior it is reputed to have rained for forty days. From that day forward the legend has persisted that if it rains on St Swithin's Day – July 15 – it will continue to pour for forty days.

The most significant work on the cathedral was carried out between 1346 and 1404 by Bishops Edington and Wykeham respectively. This involved rebuilding the Norman nave almost stone by stone and linking the Norman choir with the later retro-choir. Since then no further major construction has occurred. However, the cathedral interior has been the centre of extensive and lavish decoration. Winchester now boasts probably the finest collection of chantry chapels in any cathedral. The most ornate of these is dedicated to Cardinal Beaufort, the fifteenth

Below: Winchester Cathedral. Two kings were crowned at Winchester – Edward the Confessor and Richard the Lionheart – when the city was the capital of England.

.LIBER.

century prelate-statesman responsible for Joan of Arc's condemnation.

During the Reformation many of Winchester's treasures were seized and much of the cathedral's interior was despoiled, including St Swithin's shrine. It was eventually restored in 1962. In 1642 Winchester was again subjected to fanatical indignities: Cromwell's soldiers rode their horses up to the altar, kicked it over and then proceeded to destroy systematically as much as they could. The chantries were wrecked; the mortuary chests opened and the bones scattered on the floor and the fine organ pulled down. Since the Restoration a great deal has been done to repair the damage but much – including fourteenth century carvings – was beyond saving.

Winchester is the longest medieval church in Europe – 556 feet – and was used for the coronations of Edward the Confessor and Richard the Lionheart. Among its unique features are the retro-choir which has the most extensive medieval tiled floor in the country and the choir stalls, carved in 1308 – the oldest still in existence, likewise the wrought iron gates in the south transept.

Among the other numerous features are a twelfth century font made from black Tournai marble; a stone marking the burial place of Jane Austen; a stained glass window commemorating Izaak Walton; the mortuary chests set on the choir screens and – the cathedral's most valuable possession – an illuminated twelfth century Bible, written in Latin.

Opposite: One of the illuminated pages from the 12th century Winchester Bible, the cathedral's most treasured and valuable possession.
Opposite below: The twelve-bay nave, the largest of its kind in the world, and a detail from the 12th century font made from black Tournai marble.

Above: The Isaak Walton memorial window in Prior Thomas Silkestede's chapel. Walton, best remembered for his book the Compleat Angler, died in 1683 and was buried in the chapel.

Left: This shrine to St Swithin was donated to the cathedral in 1962. The original shrine had been destroyed by Henry VIII's commissioners in 1538.

Worcester

King John was a frequent visitor to Worcester and when he realized he was dying – from dysentry aggravated by over indulging in peaches and new cider – he asked to be buried in the church.

On October 18 1216 he died. His body was brought from Newark and laid in a plain stone coffin in front of the high altar. The Purbeck marble effigy – added sixteen years later – shows John lying between two much smaller figures. They are believed to be the Saints Oswald and Wulstan, two of Worcester's earliest bishops. The lion biting the king's sword tip symbolizes the baron's curbing of royal power with Magna Carta the year before his death. In 1529 a richly decorated tomb was erected around the coffin.

Prince Arthur, eldest son of Henry VII, is also buried at Worcester. He died at Ludlow Castle at the age of 15 and was entombed at Worcester after a lavish funeral on April 25 1502. Two years later a magnificent pinnacled chantry was built to house the tomb. It stands to the south of the high altar, just a short distance from the tomb of King John.

The cathedral itself, serenely situated on the east banks of the River Severn, dates back as far as 680 when Bosel, a priest from Whitby in Yorkshire, was consecrated as the first Bishop of Worcester. Around 983 Oswald, who served both Worcester and York as archbishop until his death, founded a Benedictine monastery on the site of the present nave. Towards the mid-eleventh century a young priest called Wulstan was admitted to the monastery. In 1062 he was appointed bishop and became the only Anglo-Saxon incumbent of such office to hold his position for any length beyond the Conquest. Wulstan in fact helped officiate at William's coronation in Westminster.

Once he was firmly established, Wulstan began an extensive building programme. Worcester was in a fairly delapidated state, having been sacked by the Danes in 1041 and left to moulder quietly ever since. One of his first tasks was the crypt and much of this still remains – the largest of its kind in England – its stout plain Norman pillars dividing the shadowy aisles.

Wulstan died in 1095 and was canonized in 1203 after various miracles had been attributed to him. This attracted pilgrims which in turn swelled the coffers. More building started, resulting in a remodelling of the choir and the construction of the richly decorated Lady Chapel. Much of its original charm and beauty survives although the stained glass and ceiling work belong to the nineteenth century.

Early in the fourteenth century it was decided to rebuild the nave and bring it more in line with the style of the cathedral's east end – itself remodelled to match the delicacy of the Lady Chapel. Work continued towards the end of the century and then stopped – for no apparent reason – along the north side of the nave. This preserved – fortunately – one of Worcester's most interesting architectural features: the twelfth century transitional Norman arches with their elaborate ornamented triforium – the upper part of the wall. As is clearly seen they differ completely from all the others.

Worcester's finest external feature is the stately fourteenth century central tower, built to replace its Norman predecessor which collapsed in 1175.

Overleaf: Looking east along the nave of Worcester Cathedral towards the High Altar.

Right: A romantic view of Worcester Cathedral, set picturesquely on the eastern banks of the River Severn.

York Minster

York is not only the largest medieval cathedral in northern Europe but it also boasts more original stained glass than any other comparable church. This includes the magnificent Old Testament east window behind the high altar, a breathtaking 78 feet by 31 feet, one of the world's biggest sheets of medieval glazing.

The cathedral was built between 1220 and 1470, two and a half centuries of dedicated craftsmanship that has resulted in a medieval masterpiece. Although restored and refurbished several times since the fifteenth century – the last major work taking place as recently as the late 1960s – York still stands firm and proud, a perpetual monument to the skill of its builders.

A simple wooden chapel once stood on the site now occupied by York. It was built for the baptism of Edwin, King of Northumbria in 627. This was replaced by a stone church which lasted until 741 when it was burnt down. The ravages of the Norman Conquest put paid to the next church. There was some desultory building during the eleventh and twelfth centuries but it was not until Walter de

Below: The massive bulk of York's east end, often compared with a sheer cliff face.

Toilets

Gray became Archbishop in 1216 that the cathedral in its present form began to take shape.

De Gray, an influential figure in the Government of Henry III, is now housed in a splendid tomb on the east side of the south transept. He is one of about a dozen archbishops buried in the cathedral. They include Richard Scrope who was beheaded in 1405 after taking part in an unsuccessful uprising against Henry IV. Soon after his death miracles were attributed to him and he was eventually canonized. His somewhat plain tomb is situated in the Lady Chapel opposite the infinitely more ornate one erected to Archbishop Bowet who died in 1423.

Another tomb of particular interest is that of Prince William of Hatfield, a younger son of Edward III. It is surmounted with an effigy of the youth, his feet resting against a crouching lion, in the north aisle of the choir.

Edward himself was married at York in January 1328 at the age of 15. Later, when he was embroiled in the Scottish wars, Edward governed England from York. The Chapter House was used by the royal chancery and baronial shields along the nave walls date from this period. The Chapter House was restored in the mid-nineteenth century but still retains much of its original grace. There is no central column supporting its immense fourteenth century painted roof, an admirable feat of medieval engineering.

York possesses many unique and fascinating architectural features but its greatest treasure is the incredible expanse of incomparable stained glass: the east window already mentioned; a soaring fourteenth century west window depicting New Testament scenes, apostles and archbishops; the Five Sisters window from 1250 in the north transept and, what is believed to be the oldest piece of stained glass in the world – a twelfth century panel in the north aisle of the nave.

Opposite: A diagonal view of York's west front, built in the first half of the 14th century, taking altogether 23 years. The towers were erected in the mid-15th century.

Left: A detail from the east window. This is one of the biggest medieval stained glass windows in existence.

Right: The south choir aisle.

Below: The 14th century Zouche Chapel.

GARDENS:
an introduction

The development of gardening in Europe was fairly late by world standards. In far away China, gardening was a craft in ancient times and, although there is evidence of gardening on Crete and in ancient Egypt, we do not really begin to learn about plants and gardening in Europe until the campaigns of Alexander the Great (356–323BC) which brought the Greeks into contact with Asia.

Most of this information comes from the writings of Theophrastus, popularly called the father of botany, who made use of the information brought back by the learned men who travelled with the armies of Alexander. In addition to the mass of description, his was the first serious attempt to classify the vast plant world. Further, his will shows that he had what would now be called a botanic garden. This he left to some of his friends so that they might continue to use it for study. The art and craft of garden design, however, does not seem to have been as highly developed by the Greeks, as it was soon to be by the Romans. Two early authors give us a great deal of information about the plants and gardens of Rome at about the time of the coming of Christianity. Pliny the naturalist (AD 23–79) produced his *Historia Naturalis* which included the natural history of plants, while his nephew, Pliny the younger, was a writer and orator, and it is from his letters that we learn about the design of Roman gardens.

Gardening had been a well-established art in many areas of the world long before it was widely practised in Europe. Below: An eighteenth century Indian painting depicts the sophisticated design of a formal Indian garden.

From the uncle we learn that the range of plants had increased since the time of Theophrastus - for example, a red rose was now in cultivation. The gardens described by the nephew were architectural and formal, the ancestors of the great gardens of the Italian Renaissance. They were also similar to the gardens built by

Above left: Detail from a Roman fresco for the Casa di Livia worked at the time of Christ. The Romans inherited much of their knowledge of gardening from the Greeks and greatly developed it.
Above: The remains of the Roman garden uncovered at Fishbourne near Chichester.

the Romans when they occupied the British Isles - an example of which, at Fishbourne, Chichester, has been uncovered.

The younger Pliny's garden in Tuscany stood high up with a view to the Appenine mountains. It was almost an extension to the rooms of the house, reached through a portico, in front of which was a terrace adorned by statuary. There was much box cut into fancy shapes, an open air dining room, a marble summer house, a fountain throwing water high into the air, while plane trees gave shade.

At about the same time that Pliny the elder wrote his natural history, another learned man Pedanios Dioscorides, produced his famous *Herbal*. This was concerned with the medicinal value of plants. And for centuries to come, the study of plant-life, which later developed into the science of botany, was devoted almost entirely to these medicinal uses. With the rise of Christianity and the development of the monastic orders, the so-called flower gardens were devoted almost entirely to producing plants of alleged medicinal value: Dioscorides' book was for centuries the standard work.

The Moslem world inherited much of the knowledge of classical civilization. For a period, Persian gardening and garden design was of a high standard. Through Persia, too, along the great silk road, passed many trees and plants from the ancient horticulture of China, such as the mulberry and peach, on their way to Europe.

Much information about gardening exists from the medieval period in Europe. Some of it is to be found in the increasing number of herbals that were published, some in poetry, such as the *Romance of the Rose* which was translated into English by Chaucer, and a great deal in the exquisite illustrations of day to day life and common objects that adorn the so-called *Book of Hours*.

These pictures show us the medieval gardens. Invariably they were small by modern standards, walled and safely enclosed from the perils of the outer world, with elaborate fountains and carved seats. There is close-clipped topiary. The flower-beds are small and laid out in geometrical patterns called knots. Within the safety of their walls the owners and their friends sit about singing and playing,

Right: It was with the Renaissance that the gardens in Europe developed to a hitherto unknown magnificence. The gardens of the Villa d'Este in Italy are a surviving example of the splendour of this period.

or making love – all dressed in their finery. Occasionally, recognised by his sober clothing, a gardener is seen going about his work. Garden tools were heavy and clumsy – spades were of wood, shod with iron.

No comparable pictures of gardens in the British Isles exist, and it is generally assumed that its castle and private gardens were not nearly so advanced as those on the Continent.

Our monastery gardens are, however, far better described and, on account of the close contacts between the monastic orders of Britain and the Continent, were very similar to them. Their principal objective was the cultivation of plants having medicinal value.

There is plenty of evidence concerning the vegetables cultivated in medieval times. Plants such as the potato were, of course, unknown and most of the plants consumed were little better than those that grew naturally wild but were presumably a little more tasty from being carefully cultivated. Some fruit, such as figs and mulberries, seem to have been quite early introductions, while the vine was also grown here at least from Roman times.

A great development in both horticulture and particularly garden design came about with the Renaissance in Italy. Gardens of hitherto unknown magnificence, and of the finest architectural quality, were made. With the great developments of international trade, plants were introduced from one continent to another. While a commanding natural view was sought, the garden itself was full of artifice - superb statuary, ingenious fountains, terraces and flights of steps.

The movement and the style spread northwards as did the great increase in knowledge of plants and their cultivation. Their impact on England can be traced to about the time of Henry VIII's meeting with Francis I at the Field of the Cloth of Gold in 1520. Cardinal Wolsey at Hampton Court commissioned the first garden on a magnificent scale in the new manner (which the King took over)

Above: Part of the gardens at Hampton Court. The first garden in Britain to be commissioned in the Renaissance style, it has been greatly changed over the centuries. However, in an attempt to re-create the atmosphere of the sixteenth-century gardens, part of the grounds have been restored to their original design.

and which the Tudor nobility emulated. Both garden design and the craft of horticulture, as well as the science of botany, developed at a phenomenal rate. Seafarers brought plants home from the temperate part of the world, particularly eastern North America. The same was happening in France from where introductions were brought over to Britain and bulbs from the Cape and plants from the Orient were often introduced through another great trading and horticulturally minded people, the Dutch.

In 1597 came John Gerard's *Herball*, largely cribbed from a work by the Belgian Dodoens, but full of his own observations on the novel plants now growing in England. Such were the South American tomato (first grown for decoration purposes) and the wrongly called African marigold from Mexico. This last was among the plunder brought back by the Spaniards when Cortez defeated the Mexicans in 1520. He found in South America that the art of gardening was an ancient one and highly developed, while the plant life was to provide us with many things, none more important that the potato which was first illustrated in England in Gerard's book. We can say that during the late sixteenth century the British first realised the extremely wide range of plants that could be grown, and became pre-eminent as a nation of plantsmen. This was signally shown in John Parkinson's *Paradisi in Sole Paradisus Terrestris* of 1629, which laid emphasis for the first time on the garden flowers 'admired for beauty' rather than on their use in medicine.

From now on gardens large and small were part of the British scene; their frequence and excellence - and, incidentally, the beauty of the mown grass - was remarked upon by travellers from abroad. More and more use was made of orangeries or conservatories to protect tender plants through the winter.

From now on the British Isles were in the main stream of international botany and horticulture, particularly when the first botanic garden at Oxford had opened

Right: The seventeenth century in England saw the development of formal topiary work making great use of clipped evergreens.

in 1621 (the first, at Padua, was begun in 1543). British botanists and gardeners travelled abroad, and such distinguished foreigners as Clusius (1526-1609) visited Britain.

In the meantime, the impetus and originality of the Renaissance had rather faded from the Italian scene, and had been transferred to France, where the design of gardens had become more elaborate and grander in scope. A new spirit was showing in the work of designers such as J. A. du Cerceau (1510-1585). Finally, André le Nôtre (1613-1700) evolved a new style of the greatest magnificence, profoundly architectural and formal in character and in accordance with the splendour of the court of the 'Sun King', Louis XIV. During the Cromwellian period, the exiled court of Charles II saw this style of garden-making, which spread over Europe as far afield as Scandinavia and Russia. On the Restoration in 1660, it was brought to this country, and became the fashion. Two great gardeners, George London (who died in 1713) and Henry Wise (1653-1738) formed a partnership as garden designers and nurserymen - their site being near where the Victoria and Albert Museum stands today - and dominated both the design and planting of the gardens of the great. The fashion was for walled gardens with elaborately patterned beds, called parterres, formed both from plants and coloured gravels. They also made great use of clipped evergreens (topiary) which like avenues and other Dutch influences was associated with the arrival of William and Mary in 1688.

At this period, garden art and craft, as well as the study of botany, was surprisingly international in character and uniform throughout Europe and indeed beyond. It was in the hands of highly skilled professionals.

In the eighteenth century a revolution originating in England took place. Brought about by philosophers and literary people such as the poet Pope, the essayist Addison and the philosopher Shaftesbury, nature and irregularity was held to be the guiding light in garden design, particularly as seen in the Italian landscape paintings of Claude and Poussin.

The revolution in taste was violent. In the hands of William Kent, Lancelot 'Capability' Brown and Humphry Repton formality was ended; straight paths and avenues were destroyed, straight canals were turned into serpentined lakes and nature was triumphant. This style was to spread all over the world, and its freedom and apparent, yet carefully contrived, naturalness is still the key to much garden design.

At the same time, interest in the plants themselves and their cultivation increased. The origins of the Royal Botanic Gardens at Kew were laid in 1759 when Princess Augusta, widow of Frederick, Prince of Wales, with the help of the Earl of Bute, instituted a botanic garden in her private grounds there. This soon became the most important botanical garden in the world, and the British - particularly the Scots - were so skilled in the following decades that their services were sought all over the world.

The greatest influence on gardens and gardening during the nineteenth century - which continues to this day - was the rapid growth of an industrial, urban civilization whose members, as their income permitted, moved out into the suburbs or even the country. Many more people had gardens, and interest in horticulture was greatly increased. In Britain this was indicated by the foundation of what is now the Royal Horticultural Society in 1804, and the publication of the first gardening periodical, *The Gardener's Magazine* in 1826.

Two of the most important events at that period were when the Horticultural Society sent David Douglas (1798-1834) in 1824 to the Pacific coast of North America whence he brought back trees, shrubs and plants to Europe which made a revolutionary change in the plants cultivated. In 1843 the Society sent

Below: In contrast to the gardens of Britain which were moving towards a more 'natural' style, the gardens of the continent, such as these gardens at Château Villandry in the Loire valley, remained highly formalised.

Above: The improvement of greenhouses in the early nineteenth century greatly extended the varieties of plants which could be cultivated in Britain. The Great Palm House at Kew, built in 1848, was the most modern and the grandest of its day.

Robert Fortune (1812-80) to China; he, too, brought back plants which are now essential commonplaces in British gardens. Phillip von Siebold (1796-1866), physician-naturalist to the Dutch East India Company, likewise brought back a multitude of plants to Holland from Japan. And there were many other collectors, including the Russians, particularly in the areas across their eastern borders.

Early in the century greenhouses were improved. For long, they had been buildings of architectural merit. Now they became functional, and for the first time were heated successfully by the simple circulation of hot water. The great palm house at Kew (1848) was an example of this development.

A great era of plant-breeding and selection of good kinds began and although the scientific principles of this were not generally known until 1900, surprising successes were achieved, particularly by Continental nurserymen.

Towards the end of the century Britain made another contribution by the development of the woodland garden in which trees, shrubs and plants, particularly bulbs such as daffodils, were naturalised. This was a logical succession to the earlier landscape gardens. In them were grown the many trees and shrubs, particularly rhododendrons and magnolias, introduced from the remoter parts of Central and Western China. First made known in Europe by French missionaries, of whom Armand David (1826–1900) was the most outstanding, and English Customs officials, such as Augustine Henry (1857-1930), these were introduced by collectors, notably E. H. Wilson (1873-1932), J. F. Rock (1884-1962) - an American - and Reginald Farrer (1880-1920). To Farrer we also largely owe that very popular twentieth-century development, the alpine garden.

The Second World War accelerated many social changes. Except in North America, the large garden became an economic impossibility while small gardens multiplied. Of the estates of the gentry of the eighteenth and nineteenth centuries, some disappeared under redevelpoment, while others were either taken over by the National Trust or opened up to the public by their owners in an attempt to preserve them. Most have been successful and today there are a variety of gardens open where the visitor can wander at his leisure for a relaxing afternoon or, for the more energetic and enthusiastic gardener, to pick up hints and tips on gardening for use in his own garden.

Alton Towers

The remarkable garden of Alton Towers, Staffordshire, hidden away in the picturesque valley of the little river Churnet, was created by the immensely rich Earl of Shrewsbury in the opening years of the nineteenth century. He engaged celebrated architects, whose designs, however, he himself often modified. Begun in 1814 and added to by his successors, his fantastic garden remains almost unaltered today.

One of the most fascinating features of the garden is the wealth of buildings and statuary on display At the head of the valley, below the lake, is a statue of the earl within a small Grecian temple bearing the inscription: 'He made the desert smile'. Nearby stands a romantically conceived imitation of Stonehenge and a series of ornate conservatories within part of which is a stony grotto. To the right of the valley stands a red building originally intended to be a 'harper's cottage'.

An ornamental canal curves along the bottom of the steep valley, the sides of which are interlaced by a network of paths and steps leading from viewpoint to viewpoint and passing a rich variety of fantastic buildings, fountains, colonnades, statuary and other garden ornaments. The trim lawns between are planted with flower beds, particularly of roses, and there is a magnificent array of conifers and other ornamental trees. But, it is in mid-June that the garden reaches the peak of its beauty with great masses of flowers of the naturalised *Rhododendron ponticum* in bloom.

However, an even more memorable sight is the exquisite Chinese pagoda rising out of a pond from the top of which a fountain plays, watering the surrounding trees. The garden is beautifully kept and secluded from the other popular features of the place. It can be viewed from an aerial railway.

Alton Towers is about a mile to the north of the well sign posted village of Alton, off the B5032 road, five miles east of Cheadle.

Below: A section of the garden in summer with the conservatory in the background. An integral part of the garden design at Alton Towers, the network of paths and steps lead the visitor from one attractive feature of the garden to another.

Above: Secluded in the depths of the valley in which Alton Towers is situated, the elegant pagoda fountain rises from a pool and throws its fountain some sixty feet into the air.
Above right: The wide variety of garden buildings and ornaments at Alton Towers caused much criticism when the garden was first designed. However, as the gardens have matured, the ornaments have become a distinctive feature of the place.
Right: Alton Towers, now a ruin, seen across the lake with some of the fine specimen trees in the foreground.

Anglesey Abbey

The first Lord Fairhaven bought this old house in 1926 and made around it a garden on the grand scale, well suited to the flat Cambridgeshire landscape with its wide horizons and spacious sky-scapes. Great use is made of sweeping vistas through trees, together with smaller, more intimate areas which are planted to give colour at varying seasons of the year. The garden is furnished with distinguished statuary, some of which comes from the original great garden at Stowe in Buckinghamshire.

On the southern side of the house is the Rose Garden where the grey walls of the house provide an effective backdrop for the delicate colours of the roses. A short walk around the east end of the building and northwards lies the Herbaceous Garden with its original semi-circular plan.

From here, by working one's way across the end of the Aboretum, with its many rare trees, and passing the informal Quarry Pool, you reach the quarter mile Emperors' Walk where, against a background of dark and silver evergreens, are set twelve busts of Roman Emperors. Halfway down this walk, a turn to the right leads across the Aboretum to enter the South Glade, a sweep of grass with trees irregularly planted on either side. At the far end lies the start of the Coronation Avenue, planted in 1937. Straight as a die, four rows of planes and horse chestnuts on either side stretch for over half a mile. Intersecting this is a path which gives a surprise view of the Circular Temple, which is reached though a dark, bosky grove. It consists of a circle of large Corinthian columns guarded by two lions couchant. Turning right down another wide, glade-like lawn, one again reaches the house.

Seasonal features are the daffodils, the Hyacinth Garden and the Dahlia Garden. There is also a Pinetum.

Anglesey Abbey, a National Trust property, is six miles north-east of Cambridge on the B1102.

Left: The house at Anglesey Abbey seen across the wide sweeping lawn. Above: A ornate Chinese style temple containing a large porphyry bowl.

Much of Anglesey Abbey's original design was arranged around Lord Fairhaven's fine collection of statuary.
Right: The Circular Temple, a collection of Corinthian columns surrounded by a yew circle with a copy of the Bernini David in the centre.

Below: The Rose Garden lying to the south-west of the house, the walls of which act as a splendid foil to the bright colours of the flowers.

Antony House

In the late eighteenth century, Cornish gardeners found that their climate enabled them to grow, out of doors, a great many plants which, elsewhere in Britain, needed winter protection under glass. This led to a type of garden particularly associated with Cornwall. Usually made in Victorian times, by one of the old Cornish families, it incorporated both the remains of the old style and the beginnings of the new, using plant introductions of the later nineteenth and early twentieth centuries.

Antony Park, with its interesting interior, was built in the early eighteenth century for Sir William Carew. However, the garden is new, the work of Sir William's successor Sir John Carew Pole, and created in 1945.

The house stands above the tidal estuary of the River Lynher, which is seen at the end of vistas framed by giant ilex trees planted in 1760. Around the house are lawns and topiary, including an extraordinary giant cone in yew. In the broad alleyway is a large maidenhair tree – the ginko – a survivor from prehistoric times. Its remains are found as fossils, and it still grows wild in China.

The new part of the garden forms an arc centred upon the house. It is typical of the modern woodland type but is differentiated by the massing of shrubs and plants usually grown in small numbers. *Pieris forrestii*, whose flaming foliage in spring is as brilliant as any flower, is an example. The hybrid *williamsii* series of camellias, originated by J. C. Williams of Caerhays by using *C. saluenense*, introduced from western China as recently as 1924, as a parent, is also widely planted as are *Rhododendron cinnabarinum* and its hybrids with their bell-like pendant flowers ranging from red through rose to orange. There, too, are masses of the lilac-blue *R. augustinii* and the giant-flowered, heavily scented Loderii hybrids. Magnolias, viburnums, embothriums (the Chilean 'Fire Bush'), Crinodendrum with their crimson lantern-like flowers as well as maples and magnolias are steadily maturing year by year.

Antony House is a National Trust property, situated five miles west of Plymouth via the Torpoint car ferry.

Below left: The colonnaded entrance to the garden enhanced by the mature growth of climbing plants. Below: The remarkable yew 'arbour' clipped to the shape of a perfect cone.

Above: Charming painted statues of a shepherd and shepherdess dating from the mid-eighteenth century stand on either side of a garden seat in the tall closely clipped yew hedge.

Right: The Burmese temple bell, a trophy of the nineteenth century Burma wars, flanked by granite lanterns from Japan.

Ascott

Though set in typical English countryside with wide views sweeping over the Vale of Aylesbury, Ascott is not a typically English garden; it is more representative of the nineteenth century Continental style.

The ground is terraced so that the view is unobstructed and on one terrace, called the Madeira Walk, the shelter is used to protect tender plants. On the lawns around the house we first notice one of the main features of the garden – the presence of many variegated and coloured-leaved forms of trees and shrubs. From this upper level the clever and extensive use of clipped evergreens to form compartments can also be seen one of which has, at its centre, a rather baroque fountain set simply in the grass.

Elsewhere is a remarkable garden in the nineteenth century French style. From a small pond of geometric design, surrounded by a gay parterre, rises a fountain from a base of dolphins that epitomises the last century.

Around it is topiary cut into cork-screws and other odd shapes. Another remarkable example of topiary will also be noticed – a sundial, spread out on a lawn, whose gnomon and hours are all cut from living evergreens.

On the other side of the house is an informal lily pool with its borders well-planted with trees and shrubs in a typically English manner.

In spring there is colour from many Japanese Cherries and massed bulbs that are naturalised.

Ascott is a National Trust property lying ½ mile east of Wing, two miles southwest of Leighton Buzzard on the south side of A418. Opening times vary from year to year.

Overleaf: The lead fountain of Venus in a shell chariot is surrounded by a clipped Golden yew hedge and a well-kept circular lawn.

Below right: The summer house at Ascott. Approached along a gravel walk, the colourful borders are always filled with seasonal planting. Below: A feature of the whole garden at Ascott is the colour contrasts in the trees and shrubs and there are many clipped evergreens.

Ashridge

A community has existed at Ashridge, Hertfordshire, since the thirteenth century when it was a monastery. After the dissolution of the monasteries, it became a royal residence. The present building dates from 1815 and to the south of it there is a level garden with numerous interesting features.

Humphry Repton carried out much work at Ashridge and is reputed to have made seventeen smaller gardens within the whole to break up the rather level overall effect. A few of these gardens remain. There is, for instance, the Monks'

Left: The grey stone buildings at Ashridge not only contrast with the other local buildings, they also provide an excellent foil for the colour of the trees and shrubs.

Below: The conservatory fronted by a lovely showing of rhododendrons and flowery borders.

Above: The terrace close to the house is treated formally with clipped yews and small box-edged beds.
Above right: The Monk's Garden was designed by Humphry Repton who carried out much work at Ashridge. This garden is next to the old cloisters of the Monk's Barn and forms a secluded and peaceful part of the main garden.

garden, which consists of a parterre surrounding a cast iron monument (recently restored). The Monks' Barn runs along one side of this garden and is divided from it by a herbaceous border. There is too, a circular rose garden surrounded by a high hedge, and also a small garden with wisterias trained as standards in front of a conservatory. The orangery has now become an integral part of the building and forms a perfect background for the small Italian garden with central fountain and fish pool. The massed planting of rhododendrons lends colour across the lawn.

A unique feature of the garden is an immense square skating pond formerly flooded in winter, now with steps leading down to the paved base. Two tree-houses or arbours nearby are unusual. Their fernery and grotto made of Hertfordshire pudding stone were added in the nineteenth century and the tunnel beyond may well have been an old ice house. To the west an avenue of Liquidambar trees planted in 1936 leads along the extremity of the garden to a hard-to-find Bible Garden – containing a small stone carving of an open Bible.

Amid the grounds of the extensive Ashridge Park, administered by the National Trust, the garden itself is owned by the Ashridge Managements Committee, the building being used as a college. It is situated on an escarpment in the Chiltern Hills, four miles north of Berkhamsted, and can be approached by a toll road from either Berkhamsted or Little Gaddesden.

Athelhampton

Dorset abounds in fine Tudor houses and Athelhampton ranks with the best. It is fortunate that in the late nineteenth century it was given a garden which matches it so perfectly that it is difficult to realise it was made 300 years after the house was completed. This harmony is partly a matter of style, partly of material, a major part of the garden having been designed as a series of formal enclosures with pavilions, terraces and walls built of Ham stone similar to that used for the house. There are two quite large rectangular gardens and two smaller ones with a circle, or corona, in the centre from which each of the others can be reached.

Long vistas have been preserved through these gardens both from north to south and from east to west but the full character and beauty of each can be seen only by entering it. There is much fine stone and iron work, several fountains and pools and a great deal of well-kept topiary, some grown to great size. One of the larger gardens is backed by a high stone terrace with flanking stone pavilions and from this some of the finest views of garden and house can be obtained.

Below: A beautifully enclosed circular pool at Athelhampton, from which point radiate various walks to other parts of the garden.

Above: One of the many long vistas through the gardens with statuary in the foreground.
Above right: Some of the large topiary specimens with the Tudor building in the background.
Right: A waterfall and a riverside walk, the banks planted with water-loving plants and overhung by trees.

The little River Piddle almost encircles Athelhampton and from the formal gardens a path leads beside the river to a very different series of gardens to the west of the house. Here the dominant feature is an ancient dove-cot standing in a large lawn and backed by a yew alley which leads diagonally back to the river. Behind this alley are well-stocked herbaceous borders and the old reed-thatched stables. A little stream crosses the lawn and its banks are planted with moisture loving plants with shrub roses beyond. Development is continuing at the present time, especially in the improvement of the river-side garden.

Athelhampton is situated one mile east of Puddletown on A35.

Belton House

Belton House, Lincolnshire, home of the Brownlow family for 300 years, is one of the finest Wren-style houses built in Britain during the Restoration period in the seventeenth century and, as the house stands on the slopes of a limestone escarpment, the garden has no affinity at all with the flat, bleak fenlands that form a large part of Lincolnshire.

The estate covers well over 600 acres. Massive and mature trees sweep in the form of a great avenue over the escarpment.

The gardens next to the house are formal. Northwards from the terrace, which has many steps, there is a fine view down an avenue of yews. The tall columnar yews are flanked by lawns with roses in box-edged parterres terminated by two half-circular, box-edged lawns.

Left: A view overlooking the formal Italianate garden at Belton House showing the clear lines of its flower beds and clipped trees.

Below left: A curved wall with a dripping fountain and pelargoniums grown in pots set in the wall niches. Below: Decorative wrought iron gates and screens leading to the stable block.

Above: The orangery or camellia house, with the ancient village church on the right.

A Cedar of Lebanon standing alone leads the eye gently to the great lawn and to a fountain and round pond setting off a classical-styled orangery, now a tea-house decorated with growing camellias.

At Belton the ancient village church forms a pleasing part of the landscape to the right of the orangery. In spite of changes, many features at Belton recall the eighteenth-century landscape tradition, including the gothic ruin near the stables, a dried-up canal, a temple, a noble-looking sundial with figures of Father Time and Cupid and the magnificent avenue of trees leading from the east up the hillside to the Bellmount tower (1750) which consists of a giant arch capped by an upper storey.

To the south-east and east the park and woodlands in the distance are landscaped in the style of Lancelot ('Capability') Brown.

Belton is 2½ miles north-east of Grantham-Lincoln A607 road.

Bicton

The gardens at Bicton consist of three distinct areas, the so-called Italian Garden, the American Garden and the Pinetum.

The first is said to have been designed in the style of Le Nôtre in the eighteenth century. It is still formal in design, with a rectangular pool, a fountain and a canal, but now Victorian in character, with its dominating Deodars and other conifers. Above it, at one end, stands the range of glasshouses with a Temple at their centre, and, somewhat detached, the handsome Palm House. These contain a most interesting range of plants all clearly labelled.

From this range of houses a good view is obtained of the formal lay-out while to the left of it is the American garden for which there was a vogue early in the last century in which were grown many trees, shrubs and plants, introduced from North America. Here too there is much to see all the year round with many fine specimens including the rare Mexican or Montezuma Pine as well as rhododendrons and azaleas in the spring.

The Pinetum, originally laid out in 1830 and subsequently added to, particularly in 1910 when many of the then new introductions from western China were added, contains one of the most remarkable collections of conifers in the British

Below: The focal point of the formal gardens at Bicton, The Temple, set at the centre of a row of glasshouses, each of which contains an interesting range of plants all clearly labelled.

Above: The elegant fountain set in the centre of the pool in the formal gardens.

Right: One of the outstanding features in the Pinetum is the long avenue of Monkey Puzzels (Araucarias) planted in 1844.

Isles. Among its sombre shades are majestic specimens of record size and rarities seldom grown elsewhere in Britain.

Beyond the Pinetum lies the Hermitage, a nineteenth century summer house covered with wooden shingles, the floor made from the knuckle-bones of deer. Delightful views of the gardens and particularly the Pinetum can be had by taking a trip on the 18 inch gauge railway.

Bicton Gardens are at East Budleigh, two and a half miles north of Budleigh Salterton on A376.

Blenheim

The original garden at Blenheim was begun in 1705, designed by Henry Wise, gardener to Queen Anne, around the magnificent Palace designed by Sir John Vanbrugh, for John Churchill, 1st Duke of Marlborough. This garden consisted of a parterre near the house and a kitchen garden some way off. The parterre was in the baroque style, still to be seen in gardens in France, Germany and Austria, but nowhere else in the British Isles. It was laid out in swirling scroll-like patterns, studded with small bushes clipped into geometrical shapes. Leading away from the house there are long, tree-lined vistas, crossed by Vanbrugh's triumphal arches.

Overleaf: One of the Bernini fountains in the Water Garden.

Towards the end of the eighteenth century, fashion in garden design swung away from formality and 'Capability' Brown in 1746 transformed the steep-sided valley by damming the little river Glyme to make the present great lake, one of the finest sheets of artificial water in Europe. The slopes of the valley were handsomely planted with trees in the style of the mid-eighteenth century.

Alas, at this time the great parterre was destroyed, but to replace this the 9th Duke of Marlborough, in 1925, employed a French master of the old formal school, Achille Duchêne, to re-plan it and thus give some idea of the original setting of the Palace. Duchêne ably complied with this and created formal gardens with ponds, fountains and parterres – one of the major delights of Blenheim and reminiscent of Versailles.

Blenheim Palace, with its extensive garden and surrounding parkland, lies in the village of Woodstock, eight miles north of Oxford on the A34.

Below left: Although much of Blenheim is laid out in the 'natural' style of 'Capability' Brown, the grounds nearest the Palace have been restored to a style more fitting to the age and design of the house.
Below: The meeting point of the two styles of garden design: the bridge was designed by the foremost architect of the eighteenth century, John Vanburgh, over a canal – later extended into an artificial lake by 'Capability' Brown.

BY THE KNOWLEDGE
OF
THE DVKE

Bodnant

The garden at Bodnant, near Conwy in North Wales, has been described as 'the finest of contemporary British gardens'. It is renowned all over the world and visited by tens of thousands of people each year. Its development was begun nearly a century ago, and was continued by the first Lady Aberconway and her son, the 2nd Lord Aberconway, who gave the garden to the National Trust in 1949.

Bodnant is now the home of the 3rd Lord Aberconway who is president of the Royal Horticultural Society. The whole garden covers nearly 90 acres and like many fine gardens is made up of a number of smaller ones. Around the house, and on the hillside immediately below, there are six great terraces, designed in the Italianate style, with lawns, pools, rose gardens, great trees and other features such as garden statuary and urns.

The terrace walls and the pergolas are clothed with plants many of them rare, others tender but flourishing in this mild, moist climate.

On the canal terrace at one end of a long, narrow, formal pool stands the Pin Mill, originally built about 1730 at Woodchester in Gloucestershire. It was once used for pin manufacture, hence its name, but was moved to its present site just

Above: The view looking southwest over Bodnant's Italianate terraces and the formal Lily pool (The Lily Terrace) to the Snowdon range.

Left: A glimpse of the woodland garden, developed in the glen, full of bright colour in May.

Above: The Pin Mill, originally used for pin manufacture in Gloucestershire, at the end of the canal, seen from the open air theatre.

before the last war and is now used as a garden house. At the other end of the canal is an open-air theatre built in the Italianate style.

Leading from the terraces, there are walks lined with rhododendrons for which Bodnant is famous, with camellias and with flowering trees. They take you to shrub gardens and down to the glory of this garden, the Dell. This is a glen in which tower many fine specimen trees, especially conifers, many of them planted nearly a century ago and through which runs the little river Hiraethlyn, its power once used to turn a flour mill. From a bridge which spans the river there are fine views along the Dell.

The banks are planted with masses of rhododendrons, particularly of the azalea section, camellias, enkianthus and other shrubs. Round the rocky pools, there are primulas and other moisture-loving plants.

Bodnant is on the east side of the Conwy Valley some four miles south of Conway and seven miles from Llandudno and Colwyn Bay. It is seven miles north of Llanrwst, on the A470 (A496) road. Visitors are admitted only at the main entrance on the Eglwysbach road, where there is a car park.

The garden is supervised by Lord Aberconway, V.M.H. for the National Trust.

Borde Hill

Borde Hill is a delightful stone-built Sussex manor house standing on a low saddle of ground a little to the north of Haywards Heath. The original garden is in the landscape style with a large lawn to the south terminated by a deep ha-ha (a dry ditch with a vertical face on the side of the lawn), permitting uninterrupted views towards the South Downs and, to the north, an entrance drive with a little terraced garden below it, which equally effectively displays the rolling, well-wooded countryside in that direction. The southern vista is flanked by trees which extend to form a woodland where the ground rises and then falls into two large dells, perhaps the sites of medieval mining operations.

Into this lovely setting a notable collection of choice plants has been introduced during the present century. Rhododendrons fill the formal beds in the terrace garden beside the drive and flank the path leading to the woodland. They also fill large parts of the woodland itself and the larger of the two dells, in the shelter of which they have grown very large. Great drifts of highly-coloured azaleas ring the main lawn and grow on the lower slopes of the woodland. At its highest point, where there is another smaller house with a little garden of its own, half-hidden in the trees and bushes, there are raised stone-edged beds and a somewhat formal design, though the whole is so heavily clothed with anthemis and other hardy plants that its formal character is almost concealed.

The second of the two dells has been developed as a water and bog garden. Here will be found the Ostrich Plume and other hardy ferns together with hostas, irises, astilbes, euphorbias, ligularias and many more plants with fine foliage to supplement their flowers.

The garden is reached on the Balcombe road over one mile north of Haywards Heath.

Below: The stone-built manor house at Borde Hill in its beautiful setting.

Above: A statue by the Italian sculptor, Antonio Tantardini, of a veiled woman.
Right: Azaleas are quite a feature of the garden and the 'Azalea Ring' is outstandingly lovely in May.

Right: Near the walled garden, where there are examples of camellias 'Donation' and 'Salutation', there is some fine topiary work.

Bramham

Why is it that Britain has no great formal gardens, architecturally designed, elaborated with terraces, canals, fountains, temples and long straight vistas on the same scale as those of Italy, France, Spain, Austria and elsewhere on the Continent? The answer is that in the early eighteenth century the English landscape garden was developed and fashion decreed that all the old gardens should be replaced by those in the new style of 'Capability' Brown. All went, except a very few that were somehow overlooked; one of these is the delightful Bramham Park, Yorkshire.

Robert Benson, later Lord Bingley, in about 1699 acquired the estate upon which Thomas Archer designed a house. Around this the garden was laid out. First came the long, straight woodland walks and the formal canals to which, up to about 1750, the buildings and ornaments were by degrees added.

The whole plan was devised in the form of simple geometry. At one point where rides intersect stands a magnificent vase, the 'Four Faces', from which there are views down a canal and up the long 'Cathedral Ride'. At one end of the broad walk in front of the house is a temple in the Ionic manner from which there is a view in retrospect to the obelisk pond, from which water pours down an elaborate cascade. A delightful octagonal 'Gothic' temple provides a view which includes the pond seen from another aspect. There are, too, carefully designed vistas over the park.

The trees, mostly beech, between which these walks passed, had become huge, their smooth grey trunks majestic. In February 1962 a devastating gale blew about 400 right over, their roots tearing up the ground. Many others were damaged. With great courage, the owners began clearing the wreckage, and then to replant. The young trees have grown well.

Bramham Park lies six miles south of Wetherby just off the A1 road.

Below: One of the canals at Bramham, one of the few original formal gardens remaining in Britain.

Above: The octagonal 'Gothic' temple, one of a number of fine garden buildings at Bramham Park.
Above right: One of the grotesque wall fountains through which water is fed into the canals.

Right: The entrance gates, flanked by sphinxes and elaborate rustic piers.

Branklyn

Branklyn is a remarkable garden, as exciting for the plantsman as it is for the amateur. The size of the garden is now two acres. In 1926 when the late John and Dorothy Renton built the house it was about a third of the size and contained but few plants and those of no great outstanding interest. It was some years before they became keenly interested, but their subsequent enthusiasm led to the gradual acquisition of an adjoining orchard until necessity or discretion called a halt when the garden had reached its present size. The things which interested them most were alpines and ericaceous plants. To accommodate these, two large scree beds were made and in due course peat walls in the shadier parts of the garden for the many gaultherias, cassiopes, vacciniums, dwarf rhododendrons and a multitude of other plants which prefer these conditions. In dealing with a small area the selection of plants is particularly important. At Branklyn each plant had to earn itself a place; rarity or cultural difficulty alone did not qualify. The same care in selection was applied to the trees and shrubs which now provide background and screening for the garden. They also contribute much to the atmosphere, which is further enhanced by a number of old apple and pear trees through which ramble roses and clematis and a notable plant of *Hydrangea petiolaris*. Where you have a choice visit the garden in late May, June or July when the majority of alpines are in flower and when meconopsis, iris, rhododendrons and lilies are at their best. The majority of shrubs and trees flower well during these months, although hoherias, hydrangeas, shrub roses and of course herbaceous plants continue well into August.

When Mr and Mrs Renton died, the property was offered in the will of John Renton to The National Trust for Scotland, in whose care it now rests.

Branklyn is within the City of Perth. It lies on the east side of the River Tay a quarter of a mile south of Queen's Bridge on the Dundee road – one of the many gardens that flourish on the 'cold', east side of Scotland.

Below: Grass is used for the paths at Branklyn, running between borders richly planted with shrubs and perennials.

Above: The collection of plants amassed at Branklyn is remarkably wide, and all are peat loving. The garden was built up during the life-time of Mr and Mrs Renton and on their death given over to the National Trust for Scotland.

Right: A number of old trees have been enveloped in roses and clematis and add to the background colour effect of the garden.

Brodick

The Isle of Arran lies in the Firth of Clyde. It is mountainous – Goat Fell rises to over 2,800 feet – though the low ground by the sea is very fertile and the Gulf Stream gives mild conditions counter-balanced by destructive winds.

By the sea on the eastern side stands Brodick Castle, a typical Scottish baronial building with mountains as a back-drop. Immediately in front of the building there is a long grass terrace with magnificent views. This leads to an old walled garden containing six rectangular lawns between which are pergolas covered with wisteria and a good selection of climbing roses. Against three of its sides are borders of herbaceous plants as well as, for example, tender fuchsia hybrids.

Below that, separated from the sea by giant bushes of *Rhododendron ponticum* which give protection against storms, is a woodland walk.

In the thirty years before her death in 1957, the Duchess of Montrose cleared and converted ancient scrub to create the famous garden we see now. Bays were cleared to shelter the sensationally large-leaved and tree-like rhododendrons, many of which were introduced from western China and Tibet by collectors such as Forrest and Kingdon-Ward. With an annual rainfall of some 70 inches a year, these giants are so at home that they seed themselves.

More recently a rock and water garden have been added and even more rhododendrons introduced from the collection of Sir James Horlick on the island of Gigha. Brodick also boasts flowering trees and shrubs of all kinds, a 30-foot hedge of crinodendron, drifts of primulas of many kinds and meconopsis in blue, yellow and pink, and water-loving irises.

Brodick Castle and its 60 acres of garden are now in the care of the National Trust for Scotland. Ferry services run from Ardrossan and Fairlie to Arran and there is a bus service to the castle gates.

Below left: In spring the primulas make a wonderful display of colour. Below: The ameliorating effect of the warm Gulf Stream on the high altitude and destructive winds allows many tender plants to flourish.

Right: Brodick Castle is a typical Scottish baronial building, standing high on the Isle of Arran.

Below: The present garden was created by the Duchess of Montrose and upon her death in 1957 the estate was given to the National Trust for Scotland. The rock and water garden have been made since that time and many varieties of rhododendrons introduced.

Burford House

Burford House on the boundary of Shropshire and Worcestershire, is in one of the most fertile parts of Britain, watered by the River Teme after it has left the border of Wales. The river flows past the garden. An early eighteenth century red-brick building, Burford House is the home of Mr John Treasure, who has made around it one of the most original and interesting of modern gardens.

It is essentially a plantsman's garden in which the contents must have great decorative value rather than botanical interest. Around the house there is a raised area treated formally. The planning of the garden itself consists of irregularly shaped beds set in wide areas of mown grass. These beds are planted, as is the whole garden, with most carefully selected shrubs and plants. Foliage and form are as important as flower, while labour-saving is very carefully considered. Many plants are grown in an unorthodox manner – for example, clematis (of which there is a remarkable selection) are often found interweaving through other plants instead of being conventionally trained. The garden and its planting is of particular practical interest to those making small or moderate sized gardens.

Burford House lies off the Worcester–Ludlow A456 road, one mile west of Tenbury Wells and nine miles east of Ludlow.

Left: The eighteenth century manor house at Burford is set in one of the most interesting of modern gardens. The canal pool on the north side of the house reflects the only formality in the garden.

Below: The church tower set beyond the shrub borders. There is a good collection of shrubs now reaching maturity.

Below left: The paved garden and pool where the only splash of colour is provided by the petunias in plant containers.

Above: The decorative use to which many plants have been put in this garden makes it one of the most interesting for plantsmen to visit. Here ivy is used to clothe the steps that break up the levels of the garden.

Right: Part of the stream garden at Burford House, a garden that makes full use of the water from the River Teme that runs through it.

Buscot Park

Buscot Park, Berkshire, is a fine example of the work of Harold Ainsworth Peto, who continued the work of William Robinson and Gertrude Jekyll in breaking away from the stuffy, over-formal style of Victorian gardening.

Peto was one of the foremost garden designers, who developed a new style of simplified classical naturalness and understood the art of planting as well as design. It was William Robinson and Gertrude Jekyll who by their example and writings brought informal gardening with herbaceous borders and naturalised plants back into vogue.

In 1787, Buscot Park was merely a 'modern' house on a hill top with a 'pretty piece of water'. Peto, who lived from 1854 to 1933, showed his genius in using the lake to make a fine water garden. The principal feature which he created is a long grass walk with a narrow canal at its centre between high trees falling in a series of stages towards the lake. The lake presents a breath-taking vista as it suddenly appears in view.

The walk by the canal is full of varied interest. At one stage there is a fountain, and at another the canal is crossed by a bridge. The canal is planted with water-lilies and at the main intersection there are fine vistas crossing the main one.

Later additions to Peto's work include a young avenue of Cypress Oaks and a group of figures – examples of modern sculpture.

Buscot Park is a National Trust property and lies three miles north-west of Faringdon on the A417 Lechlade-Faringdon road.

The principle feature of Buscot Park is the long grass walk with a narrow canal at its centre. Left: The fountain at the top of the canal walk, leads down in a series of levels to the 20 acre lake below.

Above: Fine vistas cross the main one which runs the length of the canal and are framed by well-sited trees.

Right: Water plays a major part in the garden design at Buscot Park. Here the courtyard pool reflects the statues set in niches.

Castle Howard

Horace Walpole, the eighteenth century connoisseur, described Castle Howard, Yorkshire, and its surroundings, as 'sublime'. The woods he said, were worthy of being each a metropolis of the Druids. The lawn, he called the 'noblest in the world'. Begun in 1699, for Charles, third Earl of Carlisle, by Sir John Vanbrugh, the architect and dramatist, and Nicholas Hawksmoor, the architect, the building is surrounded by the first great landscape garden in the British Isles. It is quite distinct from the largest of the formal gardens of its day, but differs greatly from the typical 'Capability' Brown landscapes that followed.

The original long terrace extends from the east end of the house with giant statues spaced out along its route. It terminates in Vanbrugh's 'Temple of the Four Winds'; beyond lies Hawksmoor's mausoleum – two landscape garden buildings probably as beautiful as anything in Europe. Walpole wrote of the mausoleum that it would 'tempt one to be buried alive'. Below lies the lake. There are other objects of architectural interest, including a bridge, which leads the eye across the park.

Close against the house to the south is a simple formal garden with clipped hedges and statuary. In the centre is a large fountain with a Victorian style statue depicting Atlas supporting the globe. Other sculpture is well placed in the vicinity of the house, including a boar in the garden against the west side. Some delightful flower borders have recently been added.

Castle Howard is reached by passing through magnificent avenues of trees lying just north of the A64 road, six miles west of Malton and fourteen miles north-east of York.

Left: The view looking across the lake towards the 'Mausoleum'. Many of the gardens buildings were designed to form focal points for the views.

Above: The classical landscape as seen from near the 'Temple'. The bridge was designed by D. Garrett in the 1740s and the 'Mausoleum' by architect and dramatist, Nicholas Hawksmoor in the 1730s.

Right: The 'Temple of the Four Winds' designed by Sir John Vanburgh between 1724–26.

Charlecote

This estate belonged to the Lucy family from the twelfth century until it was given to the National Trust in 1945; the cleft oak palings which today surround the Deer Park and can be seen from the road, are of the type that has been used since medieval times.

While walking down the long straight drive leading to the Gatehouse, the visitor will see the well-stocked park, full of red and fallow deer which Shakespeare is supposed to have poached, and the herd of Spanish sheep. Over the years the brickwork of the Gatehouse has mellowed to a rosy pink and is unaltered since Shakespearean days. The Gatehouse leads into the forecourt with herbaceous borders and two charming lead figures of a shepherd and shepherdess dating back to 1718.

Over the chimney-piece in the Drawing Room an item of interest to gardeners can be seen. It is a fine painting of Charlecote in 1696 showing the formal garden which was swept away by 'Capability' Brown when he landscaped the Park about 1760.

The long Grass Walks within a walled garden, the elaborate parterres and the curiously designed Double Canal from which arose a tall summer house reached by a long narrow path with water on either side, have disappeared. The gardens by the house today, except for 'Capability's' Lebanon Cedars that sweep the grass, are of the nineteenth century, reaching down to the River Avon. All around are views of parkland which might well be the setting for a Shakespeare comedy.

Charlecote is four miles east of Stratford-on-Avon, on the north side of B4086. Bus 518 (Stratford, Warwick, Leamington, Coventry) passes the gate. The nearest railway station is Stratford on Avon.

Below: Balustraded steps lead down to the River Avon which meanders lazily through the park at Charlecote.

Right: The exquisite statue of a shepherd set against the red-bricked Tudor gatehouse.

Below: A shepherd and his dog and a shepherdess flank stone steps, the walls surmounted by flower-filled vases.

Chartwell

It is interesting to compare the garden around Chartwell created by Sir Winston Churchill, with that of his great ancestor, Marlborough at Blenheim Palace. The palace gardens at Blenheim are among the great and lavish spectacles of British gardens.

The magnificence of Chartwell is of another kind. It belongs to the wide and very English panorama of the countryside over which it looks.

The house is set towards the head of a steepish valley. It is unusually tall, looking back, in design, more to the English yeoman's home rather than the classical splendours of Blenheim. It stands on a platform which is irregularly terraced with some formality before merging into the landscape.

The entrance from the car park passes by some rock-work with a small pool, shrubs and trees. Below the house there are pools in the valley supplied by a stream. They are the fish pond, whose golden orfe Sir Winston delighted to see, the swimming pool and the waters on which glide the famous black swans, originally a present from Australia. All these are carefully landscaped into the scene.

The garden proper lies around the house, whose height and walls are well used to shelter climbing and other plants. There are steps down to the grass below, but it is better to continue along the higher level through a series of interlinked gardens, moving on as the view over the countryside, of orchards, fields and copses reaches out further and further. The most interesting part in high summer is undoubtedly what is now a large rose garden surrounded by the wall built by Sir Winston himself. Here is the walk of golden roses given to Sir Winston and Lady Churchill by their family as a golden wedding present.

It is pleasant to walk back on the grass immediately under the house. Good use has been made of the lower terrace walls, while in the grass there are planted a number of interesting trees, such as a yellow-flowered horse-chestnut (*Aesculus octandra*) and silver maples (*Acer saccharinum*) natives of North America.

Chartwell is a National Trust property. It is two miles south of Westerham, in Kent, forking left off the B2026 after one and a half miles.

Above: An ornamental vine scrambles over a pergola to give a play of light and shade.

Left: One of the outstanding features of Chartwell in summer is the sheltered Rose Garden.

Above: A view across the stream to the lawns and rose covered wall that surrounds the house just visible in amongst the trees.

Right: The rose garden in which the gold and yellow roses contrast splendidly with the blue of Nepeta mussinii planted around the edges.

Chatsworth

At Chatsworth, the ancient seat of the Dukes of Devonshire, is to be seen a history of gardening. The present house was begun in 1687. Around it, George London and Henry Wise, the most important garden designers of the day, laid out a vast and sumptuous garden in the style that Le Nôtre used for Versailles. Its elaborate design, lying among the sombre, remote hills, amazed travellers. Traces of this garden and its fountains still exist, particularly the grand cascade (a slightly later addition) that tumbles down the hillside. Next came 'Capability' Brown, who swept much of this away in the vogue for the natural landscape – and a lovely scene he devised in the park.

Chatsworth's great day was the arrival of an unknown young man on a spring day in 1826. The 'Bachelor Duke' had chosen him at a moment's notice to become head gardener. This was the first step to fame of Sir Joseph Paxton, later to design the Crystal Palace, based on the giant conservatory he built at Chatsworth for the Duke, which was demolished after the First World War. Much else of Paxton's work remains: there is his Emperor Fountain, throwing a jet 276 feet high; the camellia house – still looking 'modern' today and with some of the original camellias he planted growing within; there is his rock garden with its giant boulders and his arboretum with its many fine old trees surviving. Everything he did was on the most magnificent scale.

Today, we find also beds of roses, herbaceous plants and trees and shrubs of the latest kinds, all faultlessly cultivated, in addition to this historic gardening surviving from the past. A tour of the gardens, entailing a pleasant walk of something over a mile, takes one from the Orangery past the colourful borders and the Sea Horse and Emperor Fountains, into the Azalea Dell, at its best in late spring, thence through the Ravine and into the Pinetum. The path continues past various ponds to the Arboretum and on to the Cascade House. From here it winds through the woods back to the house. At various points one can diverge to see the site of the Great Conservatory and other features of this historic garden.

Chatsworth lies a little way East of the village of Edensor, six miles North of Matlock, on A623.

Left: The narrow glass fruit cases designed by Joseph Paxton in the nineteenth century.

Right: The Cascade House from which the Great Cascade emanates is one of the few pieces of the garden design of London and Wise remaining at Chatsworth.

Below: The spectacular view from the Cascade House to the bottom of the steep staircase.

Chilham Castle

Chilham Castle, near Canterbury, Kent, is built on the site of an ancient fort said to have been built by the Romans around 55BC. The octagonal keep of a later castle, Norman in origin, stands nearby in its own secluded garden. However, the existing fine red-brick manor house, around which the remarkable garden was designed, is of a much later period, Jacobean, and completed in 1616.

The main gardens consist of a series of terraces connected by flights of brick stairs, with long, flower-filled borders. Each of these is backed by a wall supporting climbers of many kinds, some of which would be scarcely hardy in less sheltered places.

Below the terraces is a large lawn along the edge of which are ten yews, clipped to the shape of chessmen, and four Irish yews. These stand beside a low stone wall overlooking the park laid out by Lancelot 'Capability' Brown in the eighteenth century.

The grounds surrounding the castle are remarkable for their trees. There is an avenue of well-grown limes, and another over a mile long consisting of Spanish Chestnuts (*Castanea sativa*). Here, too, can be found an Evergreen Oak (*Quercus ilex*) planted, according to legend, on the day in 1600 when building of the house was begun, fine specimens of the Blue Cedar (*Cedrus atlantica glauca*), Lawson's Cypress, an ancient Judas Tree (*Cercis siliquastrum*), its trunk now prostrate, and very large specimens of *Cotinus coggygria* the Wig Tree or Smoke Tree. Chilham also boasts one of the oldest mulberries in England, the parent of many growing in Virginia, USA, grown from pieces taken there by one of the Digges family, who became Governor of Virginia, and many other specimen trees.

Against the south wall of the castle is a wisteria, said to be the first to be planted in this country. This and a very large Banksian Rose, nearly 150 years old, completely cover the wall.

Chilham Castle, approached through Chilham village lies five miles south-west of Canterbury, just off the A252.

Overleaf: Flights of brick steps of unusual design connect the various terraces.

Below left: Herbaceous borders backed by brick walls line the terraces at Chilham Castle. Climbing plants are grown against the walls and behind them can be seen some of the topiary specimens. Below: Looking from the terraces over the topiary chessmen to the park beyond.

Cliveden

A wide and famous view of the River Thames flowing between steep, wooded slopes seen over an immense lawn lingers in the mind's eye after a visit to the famous house and gardens at Cliveden, Buckinghamshire. The diarist, John Evelyn, described it in 1679: . . .'tis a romantic object, and the place altogether answers the most poetical description that can be made . . . on the platform is a circular view to the utmost verge of the horizon, which with the serpenting of the Thames is admirably surprising.'

This view is enjoyed from the dominating architectural feature at Cliveden, the great red brick terrace built by William Winde in 1666. Upon it now stands a handsome Victorian building. An array of shrubs and climbers is trained against the terrace and at its base is a wide, well-planted border. The view is enhanced by grey Atlas Cedars flanking the lawn and box-edged parterres of original design. Beside the lawn a delightful path winds down to the riverside.

Elsewhere there is much worth seeing, including the eighteenth century temples by Giacomo Leoni, who helped to introduce the Palladian architectural movement in Britain. A Japanese-style garden surrounds a temple-like building surmounted by a weird, fish-like figure of a monster. The garden has matured Japanese Maples, bamboos and other shrubs. A wide, grass avenue has as its focal point a glistening white, ornate fountain. There is also a water garden with a good selection of water-lilies. The shrubberies are interesting.

Cliveden is two miles north of Taplow on th B476 road to Hedsor. The road forms the northern and eastern boundaries to the grounds, the entrance being at Feathers lodge on the east side.

Below: The south front and terrace of Cliveden, constructed in 1666, overlooking an old parterre, from which a wealth of tree planting is to be seen.

Right: The pagoda used in the Great Exhibition of 1851 makes a focal point in the Japanese Garden.

Below: Magnolia and cherry trees and the old Canning Oak in the spring. The Civeden reach of the Thames can be seen beyond, as the estate enjoys a unique position on the high ground above the river.

Compton Acres

The story of this series of gardens began just after the 1914–18 War, when the late T. W. Simpson, who had built a house on the site, began to convert what was largely moorland overlooking Poole Harbour into gardens of different styles. He spent £220,000 in landscaping, importing stone and rock, garden ornaments and plants. During the Second World War, the gardens deteriorated badly but were restored by the next owner and opened to the public in 1952.

In 1964 the present owners, Mr and Mrs Brady, bought the estate and continued to open the gardens.

The Glen, Rock and Water Gardens contain a sub-tropical section with a chain of small lakes around which palms, mimosas, jacarandas, eucalyptus, bamboos and rhododendrons from the Himalayas grow. The path continues through a short tunnel to the rock garden. Here, rustic bridges cross the pools in which king carp swim among water lilies. From it can be seen the cascades which provide the water. Nearby is a viewpoint looking down the glen spread out below.

The Japanese Garden, surrounding an irregular pool, crossed by stepping stones, was built in the proper Japanese style, to the plans of a Japanese architect, using materials brought from Japan. Pagodas, carved lanterns, figures and gateways – all full of symbolic meaning – abound. The plants too, are Japanese. As a contrast there is the garden built in the Roman manner from which, past herbaceous borders, the Italian Garden is reached. It is a large canal-like pool, its surroundings highly formal and decorated with urns and statues.

Finally, there is the Palm Court with more valuable statuary and a Wishing Well into which the visitor may throw money for charity.

The gardens are in Canford Cliffs Road, midway between Bournemouth and Poole.

Left: The authentic statuary and some of the oriental planting to be seen at Compton Acres' Japanese garden.

Right: The highly formal Italian Garden with its canal-like pool decorated with urns and statues.

Below: The Rock Garden crossed with rustic bridges. The pools are filled with water lillies around which King Carp swim.

Compton Wynyates

Lying hidden in a secluded Warwickshire valley, the house at Compton Wynyates is one of the most beautiful and picturesquely situated Tudor buildings in Britain. It has always belonged to the Compton family, and is the home of its present head, the 6th Marquess of Northampton. It was the birthplace in 1632 of Henry Compton, a most remarkable and forthright character who, when he became Bishop of London in 1675, made at Fulham Palace a most remarkable collection of trees and plants, many of them first introductions from eastern North America.

This glorious house has had a chequered career, having entertained royalty, been sacked by Cromwellians, been ordered to be pulled down by its owner to help pay his debts, but saved by a steward who ignored his instructions, and later rescued and restored.

Around it the ground is levelled below the now grassy remains of old terraces. The garden, of neither great size nor age, is rectangular. It is planted more or less regularly with evergreens clipped, however, most irregularly into a variety of shapes. Among them are grown herbaceous plants and roses, while a few standard trees give added variety. Thus a comparatively modern garden adds greatly to this historic house, and is seen to great effect when looked down upon from the grassy slopes that lead up to the surrounding woods.

Compton Wynyates is just north of the B4035 Banbury – Shipston road, ten miles west of Banbury.

The estate of Compton Wynyates lies in a valley on the Warwickshire border, and is seen at its best when looked down upon from the surrounding hills.
Below: The house in late spring with tulips adding bright colour to the dark evergreens.

Above: The remarkable Tudor house stands amid clipped evergreens neatly shaped into an assortment of formal and unrelated designs.

Right: In summer the herbaceous plants and roses, together with a few standard trees, add variety to the evergreens, originally planted to make the maintenance of the garden easier.

Cotehele

The route to Cotehele lies through winding Cornish lanes, emerging under ancient sycamores. There the squat, grey medieval tower of this ancient place rises from a cluster of granite buildings. Standing on a small plateau, with the River Tamar not far away below, it is possible to see the banks on the opposite side through the tops of the trees lower down a small valley.

Near the house are conventional flower beds set in the grass. On and around the old walls, in sheltered corners, are trees and shrubs. There is the silver wattle (*Acacia dealbata*) from the Australian continent, with silvery leaves and scented yellow flowers that open early in the year. The evergreen Macartney rose (*Rosa bracteata*) (so called because it was brought from China in 1793 by Lord Macartney) climbs up a wall – a giant in every way (including its thorns) bearing its large white single flowers over a long period.

A short tunnel leads into a garden planted with greater informality. At its head a pond is the principal feature: from it a stream overflows and tumbles down the valley. On the damp margins waterside plants such as primulas, irises and gunnera, with leaves that may be six feet across, are found. Here, too, is a remarkable building with a domed roof, which is a medieval dove-cot. The banks either side are planted in a typical Cornish manner with rhododendrons, azaleas, maples, bamboos and hardy palms.

Cotehele is a National Trust property. It is situated on the west bank of the River Tamar, two miles west of Calstock by footpath or six miles by road, and 14 miles from Plymouth via the Tamar Bridge. It can also be reached from Plymouth by water.

Below left: The old dovecote or columbarium with some of the many rhododendrons which are a feature of the garden.
Below: White wisteria shrouds this door in the wall.

Above: The ancient house, made of granite, its walls supporting many plants, and part of the terraced garden.

Right: The brilliant approach to the house in spring.

Crathes

The tall grey building with its fanciful tower, so typical of Scotland, rises among the wooded coppices above the River Dee. It has a venerable history of gardening, with lime tree walks and yew hedges dating back to the eighteenth century. The remarkable garden we now see, making splendid use of a romantic setting, is largely the work of Sir James Burnett of Leys.

The grounds are divided into a series of rectangles, some of which are framed with old yew hedges, where choice and unusual, and sometimes difficult, plants will thrive.

From the range of greenhouses runs the long path to the doocot, or dove-cot. The border beside it includes the California Laurel, *Umbellularia californica*, the Tibetan Cherry with bark like highly polished mahogany, and the large Tree Peony, *Paeonia delavayi*, with dark blood-red flowers.

The approaches to the castle and the avenues are of particular interest, planted as they are with magnificent old Scots Pine, Douglas Fir, the rare Japanese Lacquer Trees, Antarctic Beeches from South America and New Zealand, the true Chinese Cotton Tree, the weeping Brewer's Spruce, and a survivor from prehistoric time, the Dawn Redwood. Crathes Castle, a property of the National Trust for Scotland, lies in Grampian, a little north of the A93, about 14 miles west of the city of Aberdeen.

Below: A view of Crathes Castle tower from the garden with its lime tree walks and yew hedges dating back to the eighteenth century.

Above and above left: The grounds of Crathes Castle are divided into a series of rectangles that are more or less regular and are planted to provide an effective arrangement of colour throughout the year.

Right: The view of the castle across the wide sweeping lawn.

Dartington Hall

Dartington Hall was built in the fourteenth century by John Holland, Duke of Exeter, a jouster of international fame. The site of his tournament ground has now been turned into a lawn set against the ruins of old buildings. On it stands an effective line of Irish Yews, the 'Twelve Apostles', while around it are some very ancient Sweet Chestnuts and on the bank above (now a series of grass terraces, so making the old Tilt Yard into an open-air theatre) is a magnificent Monterey Pine. At the end of the terrace is a great flight of steps leading through a Heath Garden.

The rest of the garden, on an undulating slope, is largely designed around a number of magnificent old trees; beeches, London planes, cedars, tulip trees, holm and Lucombe oaks, and a giant turkey oak. Among them have been planted glades of newer trees and shrubs. By the Azalea Dell is a round pond in which two swans carved in granite stand on an old cider mill; elsewhere contemporary sculpture is most effectively placed, notably Henry Moore's 'Reclining Woman'.

Walking around the wide and winding grass paths, one finds magnolias, cherries and rhododendrons as well as an exceptionally large Handkerchief Tree. This fine modern garden in a setting of ancient buildings and trees was begun after the First World War and was designed by an American, Mrs Beatrix Farrand, with later additions by Mr P. S. Cane.

Dartington Hall lies about one mile out of Totnes, Devon on the A384 in the direction of Ashburton.

Overleaf: The house, some parts of which date back to the fourteenth century, can be seen in spring through the trees.

Far left: Standing on the far side of the Tilt yard, the line of Irish yews known as the 'Twelve Apostles'. Left: A rhododendron path leads to the tower of a derelict church.

Left: A contemporary sculpture by Henry Moore is a twentieth century addition to the old garden.

East Lambrook

East Lambrook Manor in Somerset was the home of Margery Fish, the well-known gardening writer. The garden was made by Mrs Fish and her husband in 1937 round the fifteenth century house and is now preserved as a memorial to her. It is unique in that it has a true cottage atmosphere, with close and luxuriant planting.

Many rare and interesting plants are grown alongside old favourites, and the garden is a good example of natural gardening, which is popular today. Great use is made of the old walls, and foliage plays a big part in a scheme designed to be interesting at all seasons. A large variegated sycamore dominates the lawn at the back of the house, and the wide border under a high wall is always colourful. Clipped conifers and neat hedges contrast with the billowing silver foliage and branching euphorbias in the terraced garden beside the house.

There is a small silver garden facing south, and the old farm ditch, which originally separated two orchards, makes an unusual woodland garden. Here old primroses, hellebores and hardy geraniums grow under pollarded willows, while exotic plants, ornamental grasses and green flowers are cultivated in another small garden.

East Lambrook is three miles north of A303, between Ilchester and Ilminster. It is nine miles from Yeovil and 18 from Taunton.

Left: East Lambrook Manor is a sophisticated cottage garden, where first-class varieties of plants, both old-fashioned and modern, are planted closely together in a seeming confusion, yet their growth is carefully controlled.

Right: Clipped conifers form a miniature avenue with plants sprawled along the pathway.

Below: A large variegated sycamore dominates the lawn.
Below right: Close and luxuriant planting are a major feature of this garden and helps add to the friendly cottage atmosphere.

Glendurgan

This famous Cornish garden, now the property of the National Trust, gets its name from the lovely glen which it occupies. This curls downwards from the high ground on which the house stands to the tiny hamlet of Durgan on the northern side of the Helford River. It is a spot of great natural beauty, sufficiently sheltered and mild to permit the cultivation of many exotic trees and shrubs which grow here as freely as in their native countries.

On the upper lawn, near the house, the visitor is greeted by the great succulent rosettes of a Mexican Agave and in the valley below the South American evergreen, *Drimys winteri*, is planted in groves and has grown to tree-like proportions. Rhododendrons and azaleas of many kinds thrive in this valley including a large number of the more tender varieties some of which have richly fragrant flowers. On the damper ground Asiatic primulas have naturalised themselves and grow as freely as native primroses.

But in addition to its rare and beautiful plants, Glendurgan possesses an unusual interest in a garden of this type. On the steepest part of the slope below the house is a large maze formed of close-clipped laurel with a whitebeam as its centre-piece. When viewed from a distance at the far side of the valley it appears as a complex pattern and it also makes an unexpectedly formal feature in this relatively wild section of the garden.

Near the house is a large walled garden, no doubt formerly used for fruit and vegetables but now planted with flowers including many climbing plants. From this point a path leads along the top of the valley to a fine viewpoint over the river estuary.

Glendurgan is four miles south west of Falmouth, on the road to Helford Passage.

Above: The mild, sheltered climate of Glendurgan allows many exotic species to be cultivated. Here, the lawn above the valley with a fine specimen of Agave americana.
Left: The house with clumps of rhododendrons and azaleas, some of the many kinds that thrive here.

Right: One of the few formal features at Glendurgan, the Laurel maze seen from the far side of the valley. The centre point is formed by a whitebeam.

Below: In May, the grassy slopes are thick with bluebells.
Below right: In the damp atmosphere by the river, primulas (many introductions) and gunneras flourish.

Haddon Hall

The castle-like building of Haddon Hall sprawls over the end of a Derbyshire hillside with the River Wye curling below. The house itself acts as a backdrop for many climbing plants and a short flight of steps from the exquisite long gallery leads into a small, rectangular garden cut into geometrically-shaped flower beds.

This is the beginning of a very broad terrace with, on the right, a beautiful seventeenth century carved stone balustrade. To the left are hedges and minor terraces below the tree-clad rising slopes. To the right is a view down the long and beautiful south front of the house. The ground slopes steeply and interestingly in two directions, first along the side of the building and then, away from that, even more steeply to the river below. There is a wonderful view down on a series of small terrace-like gardens at different levels, linked by flights of steps and supported by walls.

The first flight is elegant and stylish, like the balustrade, and leads to a large rectangular lawn with a fountain at its centre. Great use of roses is made in this upper part of the garden. Below this the retaining walls are striking in their contrast. Upon them many plants are naturalised, others are trained against them, while interesting plants are grown in the beds at their base.

Haddon Hall is two miles south-east of Bakewell and six and a half miles north of Matlock on the A6 Buxton to Matlock road.

Left: The terraces at Haddon Hall are connected by this fine stone stairway, itself used as a support for many fine specimens of trailing plants.

Above: Full use is made of the walls of the house. These shelter and support a wide variety of climbers and other shrubs which help to provide colour and interest against the grey stone.

Above: The broad lawn is surrounded by rose beds.
Above right: A glimpse of the balustraded parapet to the top of the terrace.

Right: A vigorous clematis grows over an old mullioned window.

Hampton Court

The garden of this palace was the first in Britain to be made in the magnificent style of the Renaissance. First laid out in 1514, with sheltered alley-ways, and elaborate knots and fountains, the jealous Henry VIII acquired it from Cardinal Wolsey in 1529 and greatly enlarged and elaborated upon the original design. He had a magnificent mount, or viewpoint, constructed on a foundation of a quarter of a million bricks and surmounted it by a magnificent arbour. New flower beds surrounded by painted rails were laid out and effigies of heraldic beasts were erected. Unfortunately, none of this remains today, but pictures of it are on display in the Palace. To give an idea of what the original garden was like, a small knot garden was planted in 1924 and the initials E.R. with the date 1568 were carved on the bay window overlooking it.

Far more remains of the next phase of the garden which was designed by London and Wise for William III and Mary at the time of Wren's additions to the Palace. This is the great Fountain Garden with its avenues radiating from the magnificent portico at the centre of the east front. It is now greatly changed – there were originally several more fountains and in what is now grass was an intricate network of flower beds, or parterre.

Below: Henry VIII's Pond or Sunken Garden at Hampton Court is planted up each spring and autumn to ensure a continuous display of colour.

Above: Much of the original formal French design of Hampton Court remains, including the Canal or 'Long Water'.
Above right: A view across Henry VIII's Pond or Sunken Garden looking across to the Banqueting House.

Right: The seventeenth-century garden was replanned and restored in period style.

Another relic of this period is the maze near the lion gate. This was at one corner of an area of trees and shrubs intersected by paths winding in and out, called The Wilderness. Nearby is the tilt yard, the scene of tournaments in the time of Henry VIII, which has now been turned into a modern garden.

To the south of Wren's building lies the large Privy Garden laid out formally with paths, lawns and trees and decorated with statuary and a fountain. This, too, was much more ornate with scroll-like flower beds in the days of William and Mary. On either side the ground is raised. That on the west is an alleyway of wych elms called Queen Mary's Bower. By the foot of the steps leading to it is a gateway passing a series of small flower gardens enclosed within brick walls known as the Tudor Garden.

Hampton Court Palace lies on the North bank of the Thames not far from Kingston. It is easily reached by rail from Waterloo or by Green Line bus. It is well signposted and motorists can approach it by turning off the A3 at the Scilly Isles roundabout near Esher, or by crossing Kingston Bridge and turning left.

Harewood House

The magnificent estate of Harewood near Leeds, Yorkshire, provides outstanding examples of two entirely distinct types of garden, both typical of their period. One is a fine example of the English informal landscape of the late eighteenth century, the other is laid out on the lines of mid-Victorian formality.

In the 1840s, the then Countess of Harewood engaged Sir Charles Barry (who later laid out, in a similar style, the gardens at Shrubland, Suffolk, and Trentham, Staffordshire) to design the formal garden. The present ornate garden front in an Italian manner is linked to the landscape by means of terraces in the same florid, yet undeniably grand manner. A large fountain plays on the main level, while statuary and the vases placed around it form decoratively formal beds, colourfully planted according to the season.

The lake designed by 'Capability' Brown, visible some way off over grass and backed by banks of trees (badly damaged some years ago by a gale, but now replanted) helps to make one of his best scenic efforts. It is a delightful walk down to it, winding among old trees. Near one end of the lake a 'pleasure garden' contains a charming summer house 'guarded' by two stone owls.

Harewood lies on the A61 Leeds-Harrogate Road, eight miles north of Leeds and seven south of Harrogate.

Below left: In front of the house is a colourful formal garden designed by Sir Charles Barry. The Victorian style contrasts with the surrounding informal garden.
Below: The delightful walk beside the lake, designed by 'Capability' Brown.
Bottom: A cascade runs alongside the path which leads to the lake and is planted with the colourful azaleas.

Right: The formal garden at Harewood laid out by Sir Charles Barry, seen from the air.

Below: The Rose Garden provides a splendid colour at the edge of the lake.

Harlow Car

Not far from the centre of Harrogate, on a site of 40 acres, there has been formed, since 1948, a remarkable garden, finely landscaped and interestingly planted, the purpose of which is to demonstrate what plants and what types of gardening are possible in the bleak conditions of the north. Here, the Northern Horticultural Society is doing for its particular locality what the Royal Horticultural Society does at Wisley.

From the distinguished entrance gate, a long, wide grass 'broad walk' is bordered with shrubs and herbaceous plants. Behind those on the left are a very successful heath garden, well suited to the district, and a rock garden. Behind the beds on the right, at the top, are the glasshouses, rose beds, and a trials area.

At the bottom of this walk is a stream, crossed at the point where there is a water garden. The opposite bank slopes up and is mostly wooded, with a glimpse of a portico of Doric columns (from the old facade of Harrogate's Spa Rooms). The woodland, extending a considerable distance on either side, is under-planted with many shrubs, and further away to the right there is a promising young arboretum.

These are but the principal features of a place of great practical interest to all northern gardeners and of delight to all throughout the year.

The gardens are situated in Crag Lane, a turning off the B6162, about a mile and a half from the centre of Harrogate, on the Otley Road.

Above: The naturalized daffodils in light woodland.

Left: The gardens of the Northern Horticultural Society at Harlow Car attract thousands of visitors each year and show exactly what can be achieved in the colder conditions of the north of England. The rhododendrons and azaleas are surprisingly successful.
Overleaf: The Rose Garden.

Hidcote

Hidcote lies on the scarp of the Cotswolds between Stratford-on-Avon and Broadway with the Avon Vale spread out below.

The garden, which extends to about ten acres, is entirely the creation of an American, the late Major Lawrence Johnston, who acquired the place at the beginning of this century. It was a small bleak farmhouse with a solitary cedar in front of it and a clump of beech trees some yards away. On this unpromising site, using hedges for protection, Major Johnston made this garden which is now mature. Leading from the cedar there is a straight central alleyway passing through a series of small compartment-like gardens, each one treated differently; one for example contains red foliaged and red-flowered plants, another an alleyway which passes between twin gazebos and continues between hornbeams on trunks, the foliage closely clipped in the French manner; this is the Stilt Garden. In Mrs Winthrop's Garden, named after Major Johnston's mother, yellow predominates. A raised circular pool almost fills another small 'compartment'. The last compartment ends in a fine old gateway, through which is unexpectedly revealed a wide view over Shakespeare's country. In some of the tall, well-kept hedges several kinds of plants are used giving them a variegated appearance. These are often referred to as 'tapestry' hedges. In the Fuchsia Garden, yew, box, holly, beech and hornbeam are used in the hedges, giving different textures and colours.

Below: The design at Hidcote is very much designed compartments and as such it makes an ideal place to inspire the visitor with a garden of his own. Looking along the double mixed borders to the Cedar of Lebanon, dark-foliaged plants contrast with the roses.

Above: The Bathing Pool Garden surrounded by tall hedges, with topiary birds in the background. Above right: Part of the Pillar Garden dominated by topiary columns in clipped yew.

Right: Part of the double mixed border leading to the twin garden houses or gazebos, of which one is shown.

There is a certain amount of topiary, mainly birds, but tall columns of yew dominate the Pillar Garden.

The other main feature is a wild garden. This follows a stream that meanders down the hill, along whose sides are planted many fine trees, flowering shrubs and moisture-loving plants to make a feature as informal as the compartment gardens are formal. These two axes are linked by further small gardens.

Elsewhere there are collections of old and species roses and clematis and a wide lawn sweeping up to the old beech tree. Throughout the garden there are fine examples of planting and good specimens of unusual plants.

The garden is now owned by the National Trust. It is at Hidcote Bartrim, three miles NE of Chipping Campden, one mile E of the A46 and of the B4081.

Kew Gardens

The Royal Botanic Gardens, Kew, Surrey, covering an area of 300 acres on the south side of the River Thames, are the home of one of the most extensive collections of plants in the world. A garden for a botanical collection was started over 200 years ago by Princess Augusta, widow of the Prince of Wales who, with the help of John Stuart, the Earl of Bute, began the garden in the grounds of her home at Kew House. The garden of neighbouring Richmond House was later linked with Kew House garden, and the whole property taken over by the nation in 1841.

Sir William Chambers (1723-96), the British architect, designed a fine orangery and was also responsible for the fantastic pagoda built in the Chinese style.

There is interest all the year round at Kew, and even in winter, or on a day of unpleasant weather, it is well worth visiting the fernery and conservatory and cactus, orchid and alpine houses near the main gate. The famous rock garden is also in this part of the gardens. Near the Victorian Gate stands the 120-year old palm house, the most beautiful building incorporating glass in its construction in Britain. In spring the Rhododendron dell and nearby Azalea and Magnolia gardens are most delightful, with a fine view across the river to Syon House, seat of the Duke of Northumberland.

From this part of the garden an avenue of oaks leads to the palm house and lake, and from the pagoda you can reach the large temperate house, and the greenhouse containing a collection of Australian plants. These are some of the main features, but everywhere there is something of beauty or interest for the visitor, not excepting the new historical garden by Kew Palace.

Kew Gardens are one mile from Richmond and approached from London by bus, Underground service, or, in summer, by boat.

Below left: The temperate house at Kew which contains a remarkable and large collection of plants.
Below: The Chinese-style pagoda, designed by Sir William Chambers in the eighteenth century, is one of the more famous and eccentric features of Kew Gardens.

Above: An oriental temple seen in a perfect setting among azaleas.

Right: The Palm House at Kew, designed by Decimus Burton, one of the most beautiful buildings incorporating glass in Britain.

Killerton Park

Killerton Park is first visible as a hill which, even from a distance, is clearly seen to be planted with trees that are not usually seen in the English landscape. The hill is of acid volcanic soil in which rhododendrons and other lime-haters thrive. The climate is mild and border-line trees such as eucalyptus grow quite happily.

The Aclands have lived in the district since the early fifteenth century. It was Sir Thomas Acland, the tenth baronet, who, well aware of the excellence of his site and the fact that he could grow tender plants, began the garden just after the Napoleonic wars. He engaged a local nurseryman, Robert Veitch, a Scot. Veitch later moved to Exeter and the family firm that he established was, until the beginning of the present century, the outstanding introducer of plants from America and China.

Entering the grounds above the house (which is not open to the public), one is led below the hill, passing some exceptionally fine specimens of trees and rhododendrons scattered among the grass. Then the climb begins, passing a Victorian rustic summerhouse, called the 'Bear House' because a bear was once kept in it. The floor is laid with the knucklebones of deer. Above it is an old rock-garden below which is an Ice House dating from the mid-nineteenth century. Up on the hill, with its wide views to Dartmoor, there are several paths. There is a walk by great beech trees, below which are large cork oaks. High up, there is a rhododendron glade and on the edge of the grounds a band of azaleas in blazing colours. In spring, there are masses of daffodils. Following the guide, exceptional specimens of magnolia, many rare conifers, the flaming embothrium from South America and eucalyptus from the Australian continent may be seen.

In this mild climate there is much to be seen very early in the year, and thence onward throughout the seasons. Autumn is a particularly pleasant time to see the gardens, as the leaves of many of the trees colour beautifully before they fall.

Killerton Park, a National Trust property, is reached by a minor road (B3185) branching off to the left, seven miles north of Exeter on A38.

Left: The mild climate of Devonshire encourages luxuriant growth and tender plants to flourish at Killerton Park.

Right: In spring the natural planting of daffodils and the vista over the distant hills, extends the natural beauty of Killerton.

Below: Annuals add colour and a sense of profusion to the garden in summer.

Knightshayes

Knightshayes Court stands on a hillside overlooking the lovely valley of the River Exe. It is a site perfectly made for gardening, and successive generations have made good use of it for at least a hundred years. An avenue of large trees which sweeps up from the entrance gate encloses the drive to the house. The broad terrace accommodating the house was no doubt cut out of the hillside in Victorian times and the series of intimate gardens enclosed in thick yew hedges.

But it is during the last forty years that Knightshayes Court has acquired international fame for its rich and growing collection of exotic plants arranged with the utmost skill by Sir John and Lady Heathcote Amory. The slopes below the house have been enriched with fine trees, rhododendrons and other shrubs; a large scree bed below the formal gardens provides ideal conditions for gentians and choice alpine plants and the terrace itself has been richly planted, though one of the enclosed gardens remains, for contrast, almost completely unplanted, with only a circular pool and one white marble statue as ornament.

The main woodland garden, still in process of enlargement, lies beyond, laid out in long curving beds, built up where necessary with peat blocks and containing a vast collection of plants, including the tiny ones so often neglected in gardens of this magnitude. Among the rhododendrons, azaleas, pieris, magnolias, daphnes, and other shrubs are Dog's Tooth violets, wood-lilies, hellebores, hostas, dicentras, violets and many more.

To the west of the house a deep dell containing a pool has been surrounded by deciduous azaleas, underplanted with bluebells, a magnificent spectacle in spring.

Knightshayes lies one and a half miles north-east of Tiverton in Devon. Bus services run from Tiverton to Taunton and Minehead, and from Exeter to Minehead: alight at Bolham. The house, gardens and grounds are now managed by the National Trust.

Below left: The formal garden set below the house contrasts well with the woodland planting.
Below: A stone seat set amongst well-trimmed hedges in the formal garden.

Above: Part of the profusion of plants that make up the Woodland Garden in Spring.

Right: A series of intimate gardens enclosed by clipped yew hedges surround the house. This is a corner of the rock garden.

Lanhydrock

Unlike most Cornish gardens, Lanhydrock is not situated close to the coast, but well inland overlooking the richly wooded valley of the River Fowey. A plan shows that there was a good garden here in 1694, but the present gardens were laid out from the mid-nineteenth century onwards with considerable alterations and additions in the nineteen-thirties.

The house is reached by a long avenue of sycamores planted in 1648, and is guarded by the highly decorated seventeenth-century Gatehouse. Around this, and in front of the house itself, the gardens are formal. Neat pyramids of Irish yews arise with regularity, and tidy beds of tulips and forget-me-nots, followed later by roses, are within clipped hedges which in turn are guarded from the outside world by Victorian granite walls decorated with finials. Here will be found exceptionally fine urns modelled by Louis Ballin, Goldsmith to Louis XIV of France. Against the house itself are good specimens of the evergreen, late-flowering *Magnolia grandiflora*, a native of the south-eastern states of the USA.

Behind and above the house is the Higher Garden which contains twentieth century plantings of trees and shrubs among older specimens and through them delightful views are obtained of the house and gardens below.

There is always something to see. In early spring there are the giant-flowered *Magnolia cambellii* and *M. mollicomata*. A great variety of Himalayan and Chinese rhododendrons bloom into June, when the astonishing Japanese Dogwood (*Cornus kousa*) is a remarkable sight. Later in the season, hydrangeas are followed by rich autumn leaf-colour. At all times, fine exotic conifers, and particularly some majestic Irish yews, impart a sense of dignity.

Lanhydrock, a property of the National Trust, is two and a half miles south of Bodmin; from the A38 turn south at Carminow Cross; from Bodmin or Lostwithiel take the B3268. Bus 54 (Lostwithiel, Bodmin, Wadebridge) stops at the gate.

Below: The seventeenth century Gatehouse, the wall with its nineteenth century finials and the house set against the background of the woodland garden.

Above: One of the bronze urns, said to be the work of Louis Ballin, goldsmith to Louis XIV, surrounded by formal rose beds.
Above right: The seventeenth century gatehouse looking inwards towards the formal garden.

Right: Part of the formal garden around the house.

Montacute House

Montacute House was finished near the end of Queen Elizabeth I's reign. It is the most splendid and complete example of its kind remaining to us. The present garden bears little resemblance to the original for one reason: the present entrance side of the house was originally the back.

Near the entrance it is worth noticing two interesting trees. Both are specimens of the Monterey cypress (*Cupressus macrocarpa*); one has been kept clipped as a piece of topiary, while the other has grown into a giant, probably the biggest specimen in Britain.

Against the north end of the house is a sunken lawn garden, bordered with formal evergreens, and at its centre a fountain. Designed by R. S. Balfour in 1894, its simple lines are very effective when looked down upon from the windows above. The balustrading and the obelisk finials surmounting it so exactly match the similar features on the older walls that, with the passage of time, it is difficult to realise that they were made nearly three centuries later. By the south corner of the house, we ascend a broad flight of steps into a courtyard lying against the long and magnificent east front. At its corners are two exquisite pavilions, while the surrounding walls carry ornaments typical of the Elizabethan age, including two gazebos. There is no comparable piece of garden architecture still in existence.

Below: The elegant Elizabethan Montacute House, one of the most complete examples of this period remaining. However, there is one major difference – the original entrance of the house is now the back.

Above: The northern sunken lawn garden has a formal lily pool and fountain.
Above right: A pavilion overlooking the Courtyard Garden on the east side of the house.

Right: The Conservatory at the end of the terrace now houses ferns.

Now grassed over apart from a broad walk around it, and the walls most beautifully planted, the place is a gem, although it was originally the entrance court for the arrival and departure of carriages, rather than a garden.

Passing from it to the south side of the house, we find enclosed gardens, some of the yews in which are of considerable age.

A charming small nineteenth century conservatory built in a Tudor style stands near the north corner. In the Long Gallery there is now on permanent loan from the National Portrait Gallery, a magnificent exhibition of one hundred Elizabethan and Jacobean portraits. The house and gallery have been also recently decorated.

Montacute, a National Trust property, is four miles west of Yeovil, on the north side of A3088. Note that dogs and pushchairs are not allowed in the house or gardens, but the gardens are accessible to visitors in wheelchairs.

Mount Stewart

Mount Stewart is one of the last British gardens to be laid out in the grand manner. Although it already looks mature, the planning and planting of its 78 acres were not begun by its creator, the 7th Marchioness of Londonderry, until 1921.

Almost an island, lying between two loughs and subject to the mild airs of the Gulf Stream, this garden boasts a wide range of plants that would elsewhere be tender. Making use of the visual beauties of the scenery, formality and informality are combined in a series of gardens surrounded by woodland and inter-woven with paths, lavishly planted with rhododendrons, camellias, eucalyptuses, magnolias and a selection of other rarities.

Only some of the gardens can be described here. That on the south side of the house, and running its length, is formal and in the Italian manner, having as its main inspiration the villas Gamberaia and Caprarola, but employing planting material that was unknown in the days when these famous Italian gardens were made, the parterres containing both rare shrubs and herbaceous plants. The garden along the west side of the house, with a pergola, is otherwise sunk and enclosed by macrocarpa hedges.

To the north lie the woodland and waterside walks, with at one point an outcrop of rock around which was made a natural rock garden.

Another interesting feature, of particularly national interest, is the Shramrock Garden. It is paved, and the plan is that of a Shamrock. At its centre is a bed, the shape of the Red Hand of Ulster planted with the red-foliaged *Iresine herbstii*. The surrounding hedge carries a hunting scene in topiary work.

Mount Stewart is a National Trust property. It lies on the eastern shore of Strangford Lough, five miles south-east of Newtownards, 15 miles east of Belfast on the north side of the Belfast-Portaferry road (A20).

Left: The gardens at Mount Stewart consist of a series of gardens, some formal and others informal, skilfully created by Lady Londonderry after the First World War. The Tin-N'An Oge or Burial Ground is set out in a formal manner with paved paths and a small formal water garden at the centre.

Above: The Spanish Garden set out in formal manner is a sunken garden. Here the formal pool lies below an impressive flight of steps which leads down from the southern facade of the house, bordered by a massive hedge.

Right: Another view of the Spanish Garden, in spring, where naturalised planting marries the formal and natural styles.

Nymans

The gardens at Nymans, Sussex, are best described as a blend of formal and informal in which the trees, shrubs and plants – always of fine quality – and their arrangement play a predominant part. The garden, on well-drained, fertile sandy loam was begun by Mr Ludwig Messel eighty years ago. His friends, the famous gardeners William Robinson and Gertrude Jekyll advised and encouraged him on its development. It is a garden today with a surprising feature: the house which it surrounded is largely a burned-out shell – a true ruin of grey stone, rather than those of the artificial kind such as the follies of the eighteenth century. Strangely, the fire did little damage to the tender plants that were sheltered by the walls of the building; they now ramble inside the glass windows.

Around the house on one side are the lawns, with banks of flowering shrubs, and on the other, a walled garden with an Italian fountain at its centre, with topiary around it. A heather garden, one of the first in the country, a rose garden and a pinetum are among the other pleasant parts of the garden, in which originated that fine shrub, *Eucryphia* 'Nymansay'. This last, indeed, with its large white flowers, with golden centres in late summer, is freely planted among the sombre conifers in the pinetum. In an area curiously called a reserve garden, under Scots pines, the Chinese rhododendrons such as the huge-leaved *R. sinogrande* flourish. Past them a glade is designed to display the autumn colours of foliage and berries – enkianthus, pyracantha, *Rosa moyesii* and the Chinese Maples. Here, too, is the dense carpet of spring-flowering dwarf rhododendrons from the mountains of western China. Beyond is an area of exceptional interest called Tasmania, in which grow plants from that country and the Andes.

The gardens, now in the care of the National Trust, lie on the B2114, a little way off the A23 (London-Brighton road), one mile south of the village of Handcross, five miles south of Crawley.

The foundations of the garden at Nymans were laid in 1885 by Ludwig Messel in collaboration with some of the best gardeners of the day, such as William Robinson and Gertrude Jekyll. Today, Nymans is famous for its rhododendrons and camellias.

Right: The house at Nymans, now a National Trust property, is little more than a ruin.

Below: The stone used to construct the grey calcined walls of the house and features such as the dovecote, shown here, has weathered attractively and blends with the trees and shrubs for which Nymans is famous.

Packwood House

Packwood House is a timber Tudor building with later additions. It stands in typical Warwickshire countryside among fields, enclosed by hedges, interspersed with copses.

The garden is within a series of walled enclosures laid out in beds beautifully and gaily planted with modern plants. There is also a small, formal water garden made in the present century. These alone would make Packwood a delightful place to visit. But there is more to see of exceptional interest. There is, for instance, a long wall ending in what looks to be an unusual eighteenth century gazebo. On examination, it proves to be nothing of the sort, but a small furnace house, whose purpose was to circulate hot fumes through flues within the wall, so warming it to prevent the frosting of fruit trees such as the peaches and nectarines that were once trained against it.

Another old wall across the garden has a fine gate. On passing through it and descending a semi-circular flight of steps, one sees a series of alcoves with arched

Left: One of the main features of Packwood House is the topiary garden. Made around 1650, tradition has it that it represents the Sermon on the Mount.

Below: Spring bedding flanks the long path.

Above: The fine wrought iron gate. The series of alcoves in the wall were once used to house bee hives or skeps when they were made of perishable straw.

tops on either side. These were made to shelter the old beehives, or skeps, when they were made of perishable straw.

Even more remarkable is the walk among large, neatly clipped yews, leading to an old 'mound', a raised mound of earth whose yew-crowned top is reached by a narrow, spiralling path. There is a tradition that this group of topiary represents the Sermon on the Mount.

Packwood House, a National Trust property, is reached by taking B4439 off A34 in the village of Hockley Heath, then after one and a half miles taking a minor road to the left; this passes between the buildings (identified by a sundial on one wall).

Penshurst Place

Penshurst Place, the birthplace of Sir Philip Sidney in 1554, is a venerable building erected over a period of nearly three hundred years starting in the early thirteenth century. In front and to one side of it the garden matches it admirably, and also has an air of antiquity, though it is mostly little more than one hundred years old. It is an example of clever reconstruction of a sixteenth or seventeenth century garden, which gives the building a dignified setting.

In front of the house is a large, rectangular parterre with raised terraces on two sides. The parterre beds are large and of simple design, some outlined in box and filled with red roses. Other beds are entirely planted with box cut into low moulded slabs. A large circular basin for water-lilies, with a central bronze statue of a youth, completes the design.

A yew-enclosed alley cuts across the garden, and there are also orchards, a

Left: An alley enclosed by yew hedges and topiary.

Below left: Prunus pissardii grown as standards in the cottage garden. Below: A glimpse through the yew hedges.

Above: Looking towards the eastern wall of the garden at Penshurst Place. The garden walls date from the reign of Elizabeth I.

Right: The large rectangular parterre with raised terraces at each side from which the design can be looked down upon.

typical feature of the Kent countryside. At one point the yew alley opens out into a large rectangle almost entirely filled by a pool enclosed by low, brick walls.

The entrance drive, at right angles to the yew alley, passes between wide herbaceous borders which are backed by apple trees, and between the drive and the great parterre are little orchard gardens each enclosed in yew. It is the free use of fruit trees in a formal setting that makes the garden so unique and gives it a Kentish flavour.

Penshurst Place is in Penshurst village on the B2176 road, three miles from the A26 road from Sevenoaks.

Polesden Lacey

This Regency house stands on a chalk ridge with wide views over undulating, park-like Surrey countryside and is surrounded by wide lawns and groups of trees. Its oldest and most distinguished feature is a terraced walk backed by aged trees and a view towards Ranmore Common. This walk was greatly extended by the dramatist R. B. Sheridan and bears his name.

Around the house the more or less formal lay-out is typical of the early decades of this century, consisting of a number of distinct but connected areas forming an extension to the house. One is a Rose Garden within old brick and flint walls, against which climbers are trained. Other small gardens are surrounded by clipped yew or box hedges.

Below these is a bank descending to the extensive lawn. On this sharp slope are many shrubs, including a remarkable mass of the low, spreading Knap Hill or Pfitzer Juniper (*Juniperus media pfitzeriana*). There are many fine trees on the lawn, including some tall, slender, Grey spruces (*Picea pungens glauca*), and notable beeches.

Polesden Lacey is a National Trust property. It is two and a half miles south of Bookham station and three miles west of Dorking. It is reached from A426 by a road running south from Great Bookham. The grounds also contain an open air theatre where Shakespearian plays are performed in June and July.

Left: On an estate famous for its trees, it is refreshing to find the cottage garden atmosphere among these roses.

Above: The Regency house, now the property of the National Trust, stands on high ground and commands wide views over the surrounding Surrey hills.

Right: A formal paved path with a rose pergola is guarded by heraldic beasts at the wrought iron gate.

Rowallane

The house and garden at Rowallane, Northern Ireland, lie not far from the sea in gently undulating country with beech and pine woods. The rainfall is typical of County Down, where they assure you it rains most days but seldom for long. Plants that like high humidity and dislike summer droughts thrive. Surrounding trees give good protection from gales and the soil is acid.

Driving up the long entrance drive shows that here is a garden full of good trees and shrubs. The late Hugh Armytage-Moore, who had a flair for design and the effective placing of his plants, began making the garden in 1903. He was a clever propagator and seed raiser just when there was a flood of new arrivals from western China, sent by E. H. Wilson, George Forrest and other successful collectors. The visitor can enjoy many mature specimens of these new introductions. Near the house are two gardens enclosed by high walls, against which are trained some rather tender shrubs, such as azara and tricuspidaria.

Leaving the formal gardens, you follow wandering paths in a series of distinctive areas each enclosed by low stone walls. The Spring Garden is full of azaleas and rhododendrons – both old and new kinds – making a brilliant display, with other trees and shrubs giving an equally rich autumn colour. The Old Wood is interspersed by great outcropping slabs of rock and Scots pines, and a small stream provides moisture for many of the smaller rhododendrons, rodgersias and lysichitums. Everywhere there is a feeling of space, and a sense of surprise on seeing little-known plants – always of great garden merit and placed with great skill. There are also many fine specimens of uncommon trees, including nothofagus, species of prunus and malus, abies and picea.

Rowallane is a National Trust property, 11 miles south-east of Belfast and one mile south of Saintfield village west of the A7 road to Downpatrick.

Below left: The natural outcrop of rocks at Rowallane provides a setting for a rock garden in which many unusual plants are to be found.
Below: In spring, the garden is at the height of its attractiveness with its collection of rhododendrons, azaleas and spring flowering shrubs.

Right: The name Rowallane is derived from a Celtic word meaning outcrop of rock, and this garden near Belfast has been made in such a location. The careful planting assures colour interest throughout the season.

Below: The artistry in the planting and the selection of plants at Rowallane was the hand of the later Hugh Armytage-Moor, a successful raiser of plants.

Rudding Park

The Regency house at Rudding Park, Yorkshire, simple in design and beautifully proportioned, stands in a slightly elevated situation overlooking a calm and restrained landscape. In the foreground are aged trees in a park which has been skilfully placed against a woodland background, one of Humphry Repton's finest landscapes. The level and spacious view is an integral part of the design. The effect of flat trim lawns surrounding the house is relieved by fine old trees, some now of unusual form, and by charming vases and other garden ornaments.

As was usual at the time when such gardens were designed, the flower garden was concealed in a walled enclosure away from the views. Today, between it and the house, a transformation has been effected. Among the trees a woodland garden, with glades and grassy walks and ornaments has been created with great skill and taste. Masses of primulas and intensely blue poppies flower underneath the shrubs, which are a surprising selection – kinds one expects only in the moist, mild countries of the South West. The large-leaved Chinese species of rhododendron and similar plants which grow so heartily, are also difficult to cultivate so far north.

Rudding Park is a short distance down a right turning off the A661 road three miles from Harrogate on the way to Wetherby.

Below left: A marble urn stands in a grassy clearing where four pathways meet.
Below: Double herbaceous borders, colourful for many weeks in summer, lead to the orangery.

Right: Blue flowered plants add colour to this woodland glade after the rhododendrons have finished flowering.

Below: A double border of roses underplanted with Alchemilla mollis and other plants.

Scotney

Nature and art combine in a scene of romantic beauty at Scotney Castle, Kent. The old castle dates from the fourteenth century, with later additions. Castle and moat, mellowed by time, are matched by the mature planted trees and carefully cultivated shrubs.

The medieval remains are concealed from the arriving visitor by the more modern front entrance to the house which was built to the design of Anthony Salvin in 1837. From the terrace of the house you can see below the castle and gardens with fields and woodlands rising beyond. The approach is made all the more dramatic by a path leading down along the lip of a quarry.

The combined effect of the garden and ruins is the result of careful design and skilful planting over many years. A great deal of work was done by the aunt and uncle of the late owner, Christopher Hussey, Esq, who continued their efforts with great care and thought. There are masses of fine shrubs, such as the older hybrid rhododendrons and azaleas, now of great size. Other shrubs include kalmias and leucothoës, which were features of the typical 'American' gardens fashionable in the last century. The shrubs are offset by undulating lawns and mature specimens of such conifers as Lawson's Cypress, the Redwood and Incense Cedar, which rise majestically over the scene. A contrast is the remarkably large, spreading example of the so-called Dwarf Spruce, *Picea abies* 'Clanbrassiliana', owing its name to the first Lord Clanbrassil, who introduced it from Ireland in about 1836. There are more recent plantings of roses, perennial flowers and shrubs, and also an old ice-house, formerly used for storage.

Scotney Castle is one mile south-east of Lamberhurst on the A21 road.

Overleaf: The combined effect of the garden and the ruins at Scotney is the striking result of careful planting over many years.

Below left: The combined setting of the old castle and the more modern house, reflected in the moat.
Below: Fine shrubs and rhododendrons in particular are massed together in a woodland garden. Their profusion is offset by smooth undulating lawns.

Sheffield Park

Unlike most gardens (Westonbirt Arboretum is another) Sheffield Park was designed with the knowledge that we often have glorious days in October and that by planting many trees and shrubs, comparatively recently introduced, the brilliance of autumn colour of thrilling intensity can extend the gardener's pleasures far into the autumn. In spring, the ground sheeted with bluebells, the gardens are equally enjoyable.

The garden as we now see it was the work of A. G. Soames. It was begun in 1909. His site was a series of five lakes in a descending chain, a 'Capability' Brown landscape with which Humphry Repton had been concerned. Around them Soames planted, usually in large numbers, trees and shrubs, often used only as single specimens, to give a series of carefully composed pictures and colour-schemes. Sometimes these are pale, the colours provided by giant bushes of rhododendrons, the Angelo hybrids, raised by Soames himself.

These are followed by the heavily-scented, large-flowered white and pink Loderi rhododendrons, raised at Leonardslee. At a later season the blue of massed gentians is a famous sight. The full glory of blazing colour is left for autumn, when among the rich greens of spiring conifers – a number of them rare – every shade of crimson, red, gold and yellow, particularly from massed plantings of the North American Tupelo tree, (*Nyssa sylvatica*) is reflected in the lakes.

Sheffield Park Gardens lie midway between East Grinstead and Lewes, east of A275, five miles north-west of Uckfield.

Below: Rhododendrons, water-side irises and trees grown for their colourful foliage contrast with the sombre hues of the conifers.

Right: Massed plantings of many-coloured rhododendrons seen across the lake studded with water lilies. Tall conifers give contrast of shape.

Sissinghurst Castle

In 1930 Sissinghurst Castle was derelict and was bought by the Hon. Sir Harold Nicolson and his wife, better known as Miss Victoria Sackville-West, the author. The rigid, formal garden plan was largely the work of Sir Harold; the planting, that of Miss Sackville-West. The partnership produced the subtle garden we now see, subtle in the grouping of plants, both for architectural form and colour. Particularly this is so in the white garden.

Dominated by a silvery, weeping, willow-leaved pear, with the woolly leaves of lamb's ears, white-flowered irises, and an occasional gigantic Scots thistle, it is a highly original composition. But there are vigorous colour schemes too, particularly the plantings involving the old shrub roses. The walls shelter many climbers – a famous plant, the rose 'Mme Alfred Carriere', covers an enormous space. There is a herb garden, an old-fashioned cottage garden, and a large rose garden. And everywhere, at all seasons of the year, there are flowers.

Sissinghurst Castle is half a mile off the A262, east of Sissinghurst village. The garden now belongs to the National Trust.

Overleaf: Formality of design combined with informality of planting makes Sissinghurst outstanding. The rigid, formal plan was largely the work of Sir Harold Nicolson, the planting that of his wife.

Below: The Herb Garden at Sissinghurst. The development of this garden into compartments has enabled a subtle development of architectural form and colour.

Stourhead

Stourhead was one of the first and still is one of the greatest landscape gardens in which the English threw off the fetters of Le Nôtre's French, rigid formality. Begun by the banker, Henry Hoare, after he inherited the property in 1741, the site was a bare, desolate valley with ponds in its bottom. The banks were planted with trees and the ponds were amalgamated and extended to make the present large lake. Around it a path was devised to provide a series of carefully contrived views, recalling the Italian landscapes painted by Claude in the seventeenth century, as well as incidents and events in classical authors such as Virgil.

The most important feature is the series of ornamental buildings, of the finest quality, most carefully contrived and placed (the architect Henry Flitcroft, whose principal work was Woburn Abbey, was closely concerned with these). These are no mere 'follies', but were full of significance to the Georgians, who were imbued with the classical spirit and had travelled the Grand Tour. There are temples, the Pantheon, the Temple of Flora and the Temple of Apollo, a fine grotto, a rock arch, a 'Gothick' cottage, well-heads and various bridges.

Above: The medieval Bristol High Cross at the entrance to the gardens. This was moved from Bristol to Stourhead in 1765.
Above left: The Palladian Bridge over an arm of the lake.
Left: Stourhead in spring with the rustic cottage and a profusion of rhododendrons in the foreground.

Above: Beside the lake stands the Pantheon, built in the mid-eighteenth century.

The subsequent history of the garden concerns its planting over the centuries with what were, at the time that they were put in, novelties. Many of these, particularly the conifers, are now outstanding specimens, while the massed plantings of rhododendrons and azaleas make a magnificent setting for the temples and other buildings, reflected as they are on a calm day of early summer in the lake. Later in the summer much colour is provided by hydrangeas, while in October the autumn colouring of the trees makes Stourhead well worth a visit.

Stourhead lies just off B3092 some nine miles south of Frome in Somerset, or, from Mere on the A303, a mile westward, then just over a mile northward of B3092.

Stowe

From the early years of the eighteenth century English garden makers were searching for a new style, less formal than the French, Italian and Dutch gardens then fashionable, and corresponding more closely to a romantic conception of nature. One of the leaders of the movement was William Kent. Stowe, Buckinghamshire, was his greatest creation. At Stowe, Kent worked with Charles Bridgeman, a formalist, from whom Kent eventually took over the designing of the garden. Kent developed to the full his ideas for a series of garden landscapes, each conceived as a picture much as an artist might conceive it. This was a period when dilettante interest in classical buildings was at its height, and Kent adorned his landscapes with temples, columns, statues and bridges in the classical manner. He swept away flower beds, parterres and formal pools, replacing them with grass following the natural contours of the land, with groups and belts of trees to open up the loveliest vistas and views of artificial lakes so cunningly formed that they appeared entirely natural.

Lancelot ('Capability') Brown, who was later to design so many English gardens, worked at Stowe under Kent. Many of the eighteenth century landscape gardens were later destroyed or greatly altered, but Stowe has remained largely untouched apart from the necessary replacement of trees.

Today Stowe is a great public school and its grounds must accommodate new buildings, playing fields, a golf course and facilities for sailing and rowing, but most of these do not noticeably detract from Kent's great design which remains as inspiring and as beautiful as ever.

Stowe is about three miles north of Buckingham. The gardens are open to the public in the afternoons at Easter and for a fortnight about the end of July.

Below: The Palladian Bridge at Stowe. Much of this garden was designed at a time when the interest in classical architecture was at its height and this is reflected in the many 'Classical' temples in the grounds.

Above: One approach to Stowe is by the Oxford Avenue, over the Oxford Bridge and between the Boycott Pavilions.

Right: The gothic temple, begun before 1744 built to an eccentric triangular plan, is an early gothic revival building.

Studley Royal

Studley Royal garden in Yorkshire is designed in the old formal architectural manner in a woodland setting of great picturesque beauty. Its origin is curious. John Aislabie, the owner of the estate, was Member of Parliament for nearby Ripon, becoming Chancellor of the Exchequer. He was involved in the 'South Sea Bubble' financial disaster, lost his office, narrowly escaped imprisonment, was fined £42,000, but remained well off, with his estates untouched. Presumably, as some consolation for his disgrace, in the valley of the little River Skill, he made this formal water garden, which has remained almost unchanged. It is approached from Ripon through a magnificent park. The design is entirely geometrical, the river itself is forced into a canal, and by its side are roughly circular-shaped pools overlooked by a Classically-styled temple. Standing by the temple, looking upstream, the valley seems blocked by trees. Following the path through their dense shade you come upon an unusual view. The river widens to form a small, half-moon shaped lake. Beyond it, as a terminating focal point, is a spectacular tower dominating the ruins of Fountains Abbey. The whole aspect of the place has been changed from formal to romantic and picturesque. The reason is that John Aislabie had always wished to acquire the upper part of the valley with its ruins but he was unable to do so. It was his son William, also an ardent garden designer, who obtained the property but in his time formality was out of fashion. There are several charming ornamental buildings, notably a banqueting house on the valley side.

The estate now belongs to the West Riding of York County Council, and is four miles south-west of Ripon and nine miles north of Harrogate.

Below: The little river Skell which runs through Studley Royal provides the water for the canal. This eventually runs over a weir and broadens out to become the River Skell again. The weir is flanked by rusticated piers and twin fishing lodges.

Right: Two of the pools, with the Temple of Piety beyond, on a slight rise and tucked into the wooded hillside.

Above: In the foreground is the lead statuary piece known as The Wrestlers in front of the long straight canal and in the distance, the Temple of Piety.

Right: Dominating the scene are the majestic ruins of the Cistercian monastery, founded in 1132 by thirteen Benedictine monks from York who joined the Cistercian Order.

Tintinhull

This Somerset garden, of no great size, but making use of modern ideas in planting, is a perfect example of early twentieth century simplicity and formality, with none of the over-elaborations typical of Victorian days. The key is set by the eighteenth century West front of the house, built of almost golden-coloured stone, from the neighbouring Ham quarries. It is symmetrical on either side of a round-arched portico, from which descend steps to ground level.

The main body of the garden is around either side of a walk, leading from this door, and at right angles to the house. Steps drop down to a flagged terrace, with a low balustrade in front. Against the house stand benches and plant-filled tubs. From this terrace runs a paved walk, the flagstones laid in a simple geometrical pattern. It goes straight until it ends in a dense wall of clipped yews, which, however, gives the hint that it divides and passes to either side. Throughout its length are placed low cones of clipped box to emphasize the direct lines as it goes through the small gardens that lie on either side. The first, the Eagle Court, is immediately below the house terrace and is a brick-walled, courtyard-like lawn, the path passing out of it through a wide opening, on either side of which eagles surmount pillars.

Another smaller lawn with wider beds follows. From it shallow steps lead through an opening into a paved enclosure of yew, in the centre of which is a lilypool. This terminates the main axis. Besides this long walk, there are areas divided by clipped hedges and linked by low flights of steps, so giving interest to a flat site. One encloses a narrow, canal-like pool with a loggia at the end; in another stands a many-limbed cedar. Great use is made of plants in tubs and large ornamental pots, in a variety of shapes.

Tintinhull House, a property of the National Trust, is five miles NW of Yeovil, a little south of A303. Dogs are not allowed on the property, but wheelchairs can be provided for disabled visitors.

Above: An attractive and highly fragrant combination of red roses and white regal lilies.

Left: The water in a sparsely planted formal pool reflects light and shadow. Groups of waterlilies lead the eye to the distant pergola.

Above: The small, late seventeenth-century manor house surrounded by a beautiful garden created by the late Mrs Reiss and donated by her to the National Trust in 1954.

Right: A formal paved area, relieved by ivy-leaved 'geraniums' planted in bold containers, leads on to the informal herbaceous border with an evergreen hedge background.

Wakehurst Place

Wakehurst Place, near Ardingly, Sussex, is an Elizabethan mansion built of local sandstone. It is situated on a narrow ridge of land with deep valleys to the west and east, which drain away much of the cold air when radiation frosts occur early in spring. Because of this it has been possible to grow many plants in the garden that would normally be considered too tender for this part of Britain and a truly magnificent collection has been built up in the past 60 years or so.

Much of the planting in the upper part of the garden follows the familiar glade style, with beds of irregular size and shape permanently planted with trees and shrubs, and separated by areas of mown grass. There is also an extensive heath garden in which the heathers are pleasantly and naturally associated with other shrubs, including brooms, which survive on acid soils and with a close covering of other plants.

There are several large lakes, the one nearest to the house being flanked by an exceptionally large and well-planted rock garden, in which Japanese maples are a feature. Rhododendrons also encircle this rock garden and a path leads on past fine plantations of hydrangeas, magnolias and azaleas for which Wakehurst Place is famous.

The path then continues past more lakes and down through rhododendron woods where even after the blaze of rhododendrons has died away, much quiet colour is provided by the tree foliage, to the Ardingly brook. Up the brook valley the more energetic visitor can return by a more circuitous route.

There is also an extensive pinetum on the high ground beyond the heather garden in which grows the lovely Mexican *Pinus patula* with slender drooping needles. The Sikkim larch, with hanging branchlets, and *Picea breweriana*, Brewer's Weeping Spruce, also grow there.

The gardens, now belonging to the National Trust, are used as an extension of the Royal Botanic Gardens, Kew.

Wakehurst lies one and a half miles north-west of Ardingly, Sussex, on the B2028 road.

Left: Some of the magnificent rhododendrons, camellias, acers, conifers and broad-leaved trees, for which Wakehurst Place is famous.

Overleaf: Autumn at Wakehurst Place can be one of the most colourful times of the year.

Weston Park

Turning off the roaring, crowded Watling Street, once a Roman road now a busy motor road, the visitor to Weston Park, Salop, soon finds himself winding through one of 'Capability' Brown's finest landscapes. The beautiful Restoration house, remarkable in that it was designed by its first owner, Lady Wilbraham, stands on a terraced garden. The broad, shallow terraces are decorated with topiary and ornamental vases. The final terrace takes the form of a balustraded arc, and on it grows an Oriental Plane, planted at least three centuries ago. Some 70 feet high, the branches spread over a circumference of 130 yards. From the terraces the view lies over the park to a typical 'Capability' Brown lake disappearing among trees.

A fine walk can be had by sauntering through the long, narrow Temple Wood. Through it wind paths bordered by rhododendrons, azaleas and flowering shrubs above which rise magnificient chestnuts, oaks and pines, terminating at one of the finest pieces of English garden architecture, James Gibb's Temple of Diana. Within are an orangery, tea room and music room. Beyond this are the long, narrow Temple Pool and Gibb's exquisite Roman bridge.

Nearer the house, the greenhouses and kitchen gardens will interest the practical gardener. The superb produce is grown by the organic method.

Weston Park is on the south of the A5 road at Weston-under-Lizard, five miles from Shifnal, 12 miles from Wolverhampton and 20 from Shrewsbury.

Below: Standing on the terraced garden the fine Restoration house at Weston Park, designed by Lady Wilbraham.

Right: The Oriental Plane planted three centuries ago, today stands some 70 feet high.

Below: Lawn and rhododendron groves.
Below right: Formality was added to the house at a later date.

Westonbirt Arboretum

Westonbirt Arboretum, Gloucestershire, is not just a scientific collection of trees but an enchanting garden of ornamental woodland, interplanted with innumerable shrubs. At every season of the year it has interest for the visitor, ranging from the spectacular effect of the giant conifers, including some of the biggest in Britain, to the smaller trees and rare shrubs from all parts of the world.

In winter, for contrast, there are the brilliant red boles of the large sequoias, the dazzling white bark of birches and winter-flowering cherries. From spring into summer, for unusual and often dazzling colour, there are the brilliant blossoms of azaleas, rhododendrons, magnolias and cherries, and any number of rarities, such as the Pyrenean oak with its grey and gold catkins.

The most popular season is generally mid-October, when the old and the new glades of maples are bathed in red and golden autumn tints.

Having soil that includes an area in which lime-hating plants such as rhododendrons will thrive set among ground that suits the lime-lovers, the arboretum has a bigger variety of trees and shrubs than any tree collection in the British Isles and rarities are clearly labelled. When it was begun by Robert Holford in 1829, he laid out the ground in curving rides and broad, straight avenues so that all his trees were shown to their best effect. This policy has been followed by his successors with equal success and is now continued by the Forestry Commission, who took over the arboretum in 1956.

There are two distinct areas. On approaching the car park that to the immediate right, covering 116 acres, contains the more spectacular plantings such as the maple glades, while down a bank to the left, in Silk Wood there are 45 acres of developed arboretum.

Westonbirt Arboretum lies three miles to the south-west of Tetbury, on the A433 road to Bath.

Below left: Rhododendrons thrive at Westonbirt and add spring colour to the arboretum.
Below: Birches and conifers in Silk Wood, where the trees can best be viewed by following the main path.

Above right: In autumn the bright tints of the fading leaves contrast brilliantly with the evergreens.
Above: A group of Lobocendrus in the arboretum.

Right: Acer Glade, an area planted with maples.

Windsor

The Savill Garden was started in 1932 as a water and bog garden around one of the smaller ponds in Windsor Great Park, Berkshire. Since the garden was started it has steadily grown and now covers over twenty acres. It includes many plants popular with modern gardeners. There are some particularly fine herbaceous borders, as well as rose gardens, raised beds for rock plants, shrub borders and climbers. Although it lacks the architectural interest of a fine house, the Savill garden is nevertheless of great interest and was created by Sir Eric Savill, deputy ranger of Windsor Great Park.

For instance, a wild woodland garden of great beauty has been made in the outlying parts of the garden, and further gardens have been added to the south in the direction of Virginia Water, the largest of the lakes in the park. The original bog garden now includes another large pond specially dug to show the interest of this type of garden. A wall built of old brick provides support for climbing plants. Further features of the park include the Punch Bowl, a natural amphitheatre filled with evergreen azaleas and Japanese maples, a heather garden, a valley of deciduous azaleas and the Valley Garden, beautifully landscaped.

The Savill Garden, which is Crown property, is reached from Wick Lane via Englefield Green from the A30 road.

Below: Spring in the Saville Garden, Windsor.
Below right: The azaleas in the natural amphitheatre called the Punch Bowl.

Above: The woodland forms the background to the azaleas and shrubs.

Right: The flowering cherries in spring are a delightful feature of the garden.
Far right: An attractive combination of water and mature lakeside trees.

Right: The Saville Garden is a water and bog garden built around a lake.

Winkworth

The site of this fine tree collection in Surrey, made entirely in the present century, could hardly be bettered on a hillside curling around a large lake. Surrounded by sheltering plantations of native trees and conifers with bluebells each spring, the arboretum has been steadily extended over the years and planting continues at the present time. Though the arboretum is not formal in design, there is a pleasant diversity in the planting, some of the trees and shrubs being placed as isolated specimens, some in groups, yet others in dense plantations with wonderful autumn colour. Paths of grass or beaten soil lead down from the car park at the top of the hillside to the lower level, through a glade of azaleas which are at their best in May and a wider path follows roughly the line of the lake. There are long vistas through the trees and more open glades, but the finest comprehensive view of the arboretum is to be obtained from the far side of the lake, where there is also a car park and an alternative approach.

Cedars and Blue spruces are particularly well placed, and there is a fine collection of Mountain ash, or Sorbus, and a great many maples and sumachs for brilliant autumn leaf. Cotoneasters produce berries freely and continue their display far into the winter. Hydrangeas for late summer colour are also a feature at Winkworth; indeed this is an arboretum which can be visited with pleasure at any time of the year.

Winkworth, owned by the National Trust, is about two miles south of Godalming.

Below: Winkworth Aboretum is worth a visit at any time of the year, but is particularly beautiful at bluebell time.

Right: Some of the wide variety of maples.

Below: Japanese maples, azaleas, and, behind, larches, Douglas firs and other conifers.

Wisley

In 1878 G. F. Wilson, an amateur gardener, bought an estate of derelict woodland at Wisley in Surrey. He opened clearings, made paths and ponds, and naturalised rhododendrons, lilies, irises and many other plants. After his death in 1902 this pioneer woodland garden was given in trust to the Royal Horticultural Society. Now extended to some 150 acres, practically every kind of gardening, ornamental and utilitarian, possible in Britain is displayed and studied. Near the entrance are the laboratories against whose sheltered walls tender plants are grown. Nearby are lawns with seasonally planted beds. Ahead is the range of glass houses, running due west, sheltering plants that range from the barely tender to tropical orchids.

To their south lie the mixed borders where shrubs and other plants are grown together in a practical arrangement. During the summer, the rose garden westward of this should be visited: through this are the fruit gardens.

Particularly in spring and early summer the wide grass path through the mixed borders should be followed up hill. It passes through massed azaleas and rhododendrons. To its left lies Battlestone Hill with paths winding among camellias, rhododendrons and similar shrubs. To the right of the broad walk are ornamental cherries.

The alpine meadow (with masses of tiny daffodils in spring), the world famous rock garden and the wild garden are reached by proceeding due west along the line of glass houses. From the wild garden the heath garden lies to the north-west. This merges with Seven Acres, a spacious planting of trees and shrubs around a large pool.

The long herbaceous borders (with the trials gardens on their left) are seen half-right from the laboratory. At their end, Seven Acres lies to the left and the large pinetum – a collection of conifers – to the right. Through this is Howard's Field, an example of planting on extremely dry, sandy soil that cannot be watered.

The gardens lie just off the A3 between Ripley and Cobham, 20 miles from London. Green Line Coach 715 runs within five minutes walk, taking about one hour 20 minutes from London. Enquire times from London Transport Executive.

Left: A stream meanders through the rock garden, ablaze with spring colour.

Above: A view of the Royal Horticultural Society's wild garden in Surrey. In such a natural, labour-saving setting, many plants such as primulas, lilies and ferns flourish.

Right: A view of the alpine meadow and rock garden from the wild garden. Primulas and bog plants flourish by the stream.

Wrest Park

The present house at Wrest Park, Bedfordshire, was built in an ornate French style early in the last century. The level garden viewed from the terrace was begun in 1706 and altered several times afterwards to fit in with changing fashions.

Immediately in front of the terrace are colourful parterre beds and an ornate marble fountain in the French style. In the distance across lawns, can be seen the Long Water, an original feature, which is a straight, formal canal between high trees with a domed pavilion at one end. The best introduction to the garden is first to walk down to this attractive building. It was planned by William Archer, who also designed the monumental cascade pavilion at Chatsworth, Derbyshire. The pavilion at Wrest Park is decorated inside with trompe l'oeil work, consisting of figures and architectural decorations painted on the flat but made to appear quite solid-looking.

Entrances to a surrounding wood lead away from the canal. The wood contains a complex network of paths arranged for the most part geometrically, but including many that meander in an almost maze-like and apparently aimless way. By following them, all kinds of interesting discoveries are made. One terminates at a Roman altar, another with a vase. A third ends at a small summer-house, others lead to monuments. Emerging into the open, stretches of water come into view – a narrow, irregular lake surrounds the whole woodland area. In one place it is crossed by a Chinese-style bridge built in 1874.

Nearer the house is a handsome Palladian bowling-green pavilion made in 1735, a fine orangery in the French manner built in 1836 and a rustic bath house and late eighteenth-century bridge.

Wrest Park, now the property of the National Institute of Agricultural Engineering, is at Silsoe, ten miles north of Luton on the A6 Bedford Road.

Left: The bath house, recently restored, stands in a secluded part of the garden at Wrest Park.

Right: The formal canal with the pavilion beyond forms the access to the garden.

Below: The parterre with the orangery and the bowling-green pavilion beyond stress the formality of this section of the garden.